# The Psychology of Flight
# Flight
# By Alex Varney

# Preface by
# Thomas Block

Other Books by Thomas Block

Captain
Open Skies
Skyfall
Airship Nine
Orbit
Forced Landing
Mayday

See the author's website at:
www.ThomasBlockNovels.com

# Preface
# by Thomas Block

*Thomas Block has been a pilot for nearly 60 years, beginning with Piper J3 Cubs as a teenager. Over the next few years he flew various general aviation aircraft and eventually stepped into airliners. He has accumulated a total of 31,000 hours of flight time. His airline flying career spanned a 36 year period, starting with piston powered propeller airliners on domestic routes and finishing with Trans-Atlantic Widebody jets.*

*In addition, he has been a noted aviation author of books and magazine articles, including 24 years as a columnist and features writer for FLYING Magazine, a dozen-plus years with Cessna Flyer and Piper Flyer magazines, 10 years as a columnist for Plane & Pilot Magazine, plus various other publications.*

*He has written a number of aviation theme novels, many of which have gone on to bestseller status around the world; one of his novels was made into a movie in the United States, and one was performed as a serial radio drama in Japan. He has traveled the world extensively for his magazine and book research, and has accumulated cockpit time in everything from blimps, gliders, and up through Supersonic Transports.*

*In recent years he has turned to audio book production and narration, and, while he has produced a large mix of material, he has often concentrated on aviation theme novels and non-fiction works - including this book. To learn more, visit his website at:*

*www.ThomasBlockNovels.com*

I don't remember when I initially acquired my personal

copy of *The Psychology of Flight* by Alex Varney, but I do know that it was in my teenage years not long after my first solo on my sixteenth birthday, and not many years after this fabulous book made its first appearance. Everything that was said in this book made such sense to me that it was as if a bright light was suddenly turned on in a shadowy room - I could now see what he was telling me so darn clearly.

This is not the sort of book that you should read only once, not just because there is so much inside it, but also because we need refresher training now and again in this most important of all aviation related subjects: basically, a pilot's inner workings.

I've put this book back into print after so many years of absence because I firmly believe that *The Psychology of Flight* can provide modern pilots - everyone from new students to seasoned professionals - what's needed to continuously make themselves ready for whatever the piloting tasks ahead might be. In essence, it's nothing less than an exquisitely written 'Checklist for the Self'.

While it's important to study and understand the rules, the procedures and the particulars of each airplane you get into, it is even more important to have a good understanding of the inner workings of the flesh and blood person who will be pushing the levers, pressing the switches, turning the wheels and making the decisions that affect the course of these technological marvels that are airplanes. You.

Keep this book on a convenient shelf to be pulled down periodically for recurrent proficiency in the area that is ultimately the most important of all: before we can control an airplane with the necessary skills and consistency, we also need to understand how to control ourselves. I think this book can help you accomplish that goal, because I know that it helped me.

Thomas Block

# Foreword

All of us desire to make our actions effective because success in any walk of life demands effective action. But it often seems that the harder we try to act effectively in the critical moments of life when we are under pressure, the more certain we seem to be doomed to fail.

Our emotions often betray us in a heartbreaking manner when the chips are down and the stakes are high. We can't turn on confidence as we snap on a light switch any more than we can fight our way to sleep.

Common-sense leads you and me to act with a reasonable amount of effectiveness in most of the ordinary situations in life, just as almost any capable pilot can climb into a multi-engine bomber, get it off the ground, and fly it in good weather under ideal conditions. Common-sense enables him to figure out how the controls and the various gadgets operate.

However, if he intends to pilot this multi-engine bomber through critical weather in a safe, efficient manner, he will study this complicated machine to learn more about it.

In our journey through life, we continually stumble upon ways of making our actions effective, just as the pilot who climbed into the bomber with little detailed knowledge of the airplane learned more about it as he continued to fly. But we need not leave such learning entirely to chance—to the chance that may mar our lives. We can prepare for effective action through a study of our nervous system and our emotions to learn how and why we respond as we do to the stimuli arising from our environment.

In this book, we will observe the airplane pilot in situations where he encounters baffling problems of adjustment in such dramatic fashion that we may learn to understand the factors that influence his behavior.

This study is the most fascinating any man can make because it can become the passport to success in all that he undertakes.

I want to mention here my appreciation to the C.A.A. and to the C.A.B. for their co-operation in furnishing me with generous amounts of statistical material to aid me in my research and to thank Dr. Ivan Benson and Dr. J. P. Guilford for the encouragement that they have given me. The manuscript was read carefully by these eminent authorities, and they made helpful suggestions which ensured sound psychological principles.

ALEX VARNEY

# 1
# Why Pilots Behave as They Do

Nearly getting killed started me on a little research.

Had I been killed that day, it would have been my own fault. It was back in the late winter of 1922. I was operating a flying school and was taking up for his first flying lesson a skinny, intellectual-looking little runt of about half my weight.

He was no match for me physically, yet in the clouds he was to overpower me and nearly end both our lives.

I gave him the usual lackadaisical indoctrination that was used in those days in place of a thorough pre-flight course of instruction.

It was a cold wintry day. I spit my words out in Winchell style.

Pointing to the control stick, I said, "This is the control stick. Push it ahead to put the nose down. Pull it back to bring the nose up. Push it to the left to put the left wing down. Push it to the right to put the right down."

I pointed to the rudder bar. "Push forward with your right foot when you want to turn to the right. Push forward with the left foot to turn left.

"That's all there is to it. I'll handle the throttle. I'll take off and climb to about three thousand feet where it is nice and smooth and then turn the controls over to you."

At three thousand feet he took the controls in response to my signal and began to pull the old trainer up into an angle of climb that would have been optimistic for an airplane of modern vintage. I bellowed into the speaking tube, "Put the nose down!"

He did—and how. He shoved the stick ahead with such

gusto that the airplane headed straight for the earth. I was momentarily lifted from the seat, tightly against my safety belt.

"Hey!" I shouted into the speaking tube. "Ease back on the stick!"

There was no response. Shouting the command again, I turned around to look at my student. He was staring straight ahead. His eyes seemed to stand out from his white face, and the dilated pupils were about the size of a dime.

Instantly I grasped my own control stick. It was immovable as if it were set in concrete. With all my strength, I pulled, but I couldn't budge it. I thought of rapping him on the head and probably would have done so had there been some solid object such as a fire extinguisher within reach.

Down . . . down . . . down, we went, the snow-covered earth rushing up to meet us. Fortunately that old Jenny had a lot of structural parts sticking out into the air. Soon the resistance of these parts equaled the pull of gravity. The old Jenny reached its terminal velocity and, with no further increase in our rate of descent, my stomach and other internal organs sank back to their normal position in my body.

Although we were still headed straight for the ground, we had the feeling that we were hanging suspended in space. As I tugged at the control stick, I was relieved to find the pressure against me relaxing. My student, too, must have found his fear subsiding, for his grip on the stick diminished as the acceleration ceased. When finally I leveled the airplane out, we were skimming along scarcely fifty feet above the tree tops.

At the supper table I was silent. I had a problem. This young man had turned over to me a rather nice collection of steel engravings of some of our better-known presidents when he had signed up for his flying course. I was loath to part with these works of art on the green oblong paper put out by the United States Treasury.

I balked at washing him out, for I took great pride in boasting, "I can teach anyone to fly." My flying school catalog contained this simple statement: "If your vision is sufficiently acute to enable you to read this catalog, you can see well enough to fly an airplane."

The next morning was one of those warm, foggy mornings of late winter, when spring seems to be heralding its approach. Underfoot, the snow was melting. I knew the fog would hang on all day. There would be no flying.

I decided to take the day off and try to learn why fear had provided that skinny little runt with the strength to overpower me.

I learned that when one knows what to do in an emergency, when there is a clear plan for action in his mind, he does not succumb to fear. Instead he uses the power and strength that fear marshals for him to solve his problem quickly and effectively.

That student froze to the controls because he did not know what else to do. He reverted to a pattern of primitive reflexes in an effort to seek security. In his case the primitive reflexes defeated their purpose as they often do because they were obsolete in the situation that prompted them. His action was directed by one of our most powerful emotions—fear.

An emotion might be described as our total feeling at the moment, the sum total of all the stimuli bombarding us from without and from within. We do not get angry in a finger or a leg alone, we get angry all over. Emotions tend to produce total effects—either they marshal the resources of the body for the production of energy, or they direct the restoring and the conserving of the body's resources, thus tending toward a relaxed state.

We have two types of emotions. We have the sympathetic emotions, so named because they cause impulses to flow out over the entire sympathetic nervous system, where each response they evoke contributes in some way to prepare the body to put forth powerful effective action.

Sympathetic emotions cause the liver to convert its stored glycogen to glucose and pour it into the blood stream, thus enriching the blood with fuel for the production of energy. The

11

rate of respiration is increased, thereby enriching the blood with oxygen, which is also needed for the production of energy.

Adrenin pours into the blood from the adrenal glands at an increased rate. Adrenin amplifies sympathetic excitation and also counteracts the by-products of metabolism that gather in the junctions between the nerve ends and the muscle fibers to produce fatigue. Adrenin gives the muscles the green light for action.

The smooth muscles in the digestive tract relax, so that no energy is used for activities that are not essential to the emergency. Tiny muscles that encircle the blood vessels in the visceral area contract, constricting those blood vessels, while similar muscle fibers that encircle blood vessels that lead to the skeletal muscles and the heart relax, thus dilating those blood vessels. The flow of blood is directed to the points where action is likely to be called for. Since the visceral area is a literal swamp of small blood vessels, the total effect is to constrict a greater number of blood vessels than are dilated; hence the blood pressure is increased.

The pulse rate is also increased so that the blood enriched with all the factors essential for the production of energy circulates at an increased speed and at higher pressure and is directed to the points where it will be needed to support action.

Fear, anger, and rage are typical sympathetic emotions. These emotions prepare the body to meet an emergency.

The parasympathetic emotions give the all-clear signal, returning the body to its normal peacetime activities of restoring and conserving its resources. They are so named because they cause impulses to flow out over parts of the parasympathetic nervous system. Contentment and resignation are typical parasympathetic emotions.

Suppose we think of our emotions as though they were news programs that are broadcast over these two networks, the sympathetic network and the parasympathetic network.

We will think of the thalamic area in the center of the brain as the studios where these programs are developed from the incoming news.

Nerves from our external sensory receptors and from receptors within our bodies lead to those studios, so that bits of news are continually flowing in, keeping the news analysts in the studios informed concerning the changes that are taking place, both in the external environment and in the internal environment of the body.

To extend our analogy even more, we can think of the analysts that develop the sympathetic emotional programs from the incoming news as New Deal Democrats of the Roosevelt period, and we can think of the analysts that develop the parasympathetic emotional programs as Republicans of that same decade.

Suppose the news flowing in seems to indicate that some sort of an emergency is imminent? The Democratic analysts get busy and appropriate millions of units of energy in the form of some sympathetic emotion such as fear or anger. Messages are immediately broadcast over the entire sympathetic network to marshal all this energy, at the same time giving the various spending agencies—the muscles—the green light for an orgy of spending.

In the meantime, the Republican analysts of the para-sympathetic nervous system are alarmed lest the body be so depleted of energy that it will become bankrupt. They scan the incoming news for stimuli that seem to indicate that the emergency has passed. From such news they build a parasympathetic emotional program and broadcast it over part or all of the parasympathetic network. Their parasympathetic programs take the form of some such emotion as contentment or satisfaction which causes the body to relax and return to its normal peacetime activities, putting an end to the excess of spending. These Republican programs direct the conservation and the restoring of the body's resources.

Even though the emergency is not over, the Republican analysts may interpret the news to indicate that the situation is so hopeless that it is useless to spend any more energy on a lost cause. They will then develop an emotion such as resignation.

While this has been taking place, all these bits of news have been relayed to the cerebral cortex on the top floor above the thalamic area of the studios. Suppose we compare the intellect to a sort of combined censor, commentator, and supreme court with libraries, institutions for learning, research foundations, all available for its use. The intellect can gather and compare all the data available concerning situations comparable to the situation that seems to be indicated by the news.

With such a mass of data available for comparison, the intellect is able to gain a far more accurate insight into the situation and to formulate better decisions than can the emotions. The insight and decisions reached by our intellect are sent down to the studios and often cause drastic changes in the emotional program that is being broadcast.

However, you know how it is in a busy studio. These programs, which we call emotions, are whipped together on the spur of the moment, the analysts calling the play just as it appears to them, so the emotional program is likely to be broadcast without waiting for any insight or decision from the intellect.

Of course, retractions may be made and the emotional program may be altered when such insight or decision is finally received. Unfortunately, our intellect listens in on the emotional broadcasts of both networks, and our intellect may get a biased view of the situation instead of considering it in the light of the actual facts. Consequently, the associations made by the intellect and the data it recalls for such associations may be related to a situation that is not consistent with the facts—all because of the hasty improvisations of the analysts in the studios.

That is why the emotions so frequently get the upper hand over the intellect. The emotion gets there "fustes' with the mostes' ' —it gives us our first impression and these first impressions are likely to set the trend that our intellect will take in making its associations.

Fortunately, the situation is not hopeless. Again we will use an analogy, this time comparing the intellect to the supreme court. As you know, the supreme court is able to reach decisions quickly where decisions concerning some situation of a similar character are available among the records.

It is much the same with our intellect. Insight and decisions are reached rapidly where there have been associations and decisions of the same nature in the past that can be immediately recalled.

When the intellectual insight or decision comes quickly, it may become a vital part of the data from which the analysts develop the emotional program—or such insight and decisions may be handed down before the emotion has had time to grow, so that the emotion is toned to the concepts of the intellect.

However, since many of us seldom appeal to the intellect for a decision, our intellects have so few past decisions available for reference that considerable deliberation is necessary before any insight is gained or a decision reached. The workings of such intellects are greatly influenced by the emotions, for the emotion grows in strength while this deliberation is taking place.

As a result of conflict the emotions may grow to such strength that the intellect may be forced to take a hand to resolve such conflict lest emotional tension damage the body. Forced to make such findings under pressure, the intellect may come up with some illogical fantasy or other defense mechanism that does not enable us to adjust to our environment but simply provides an escape for high emotional tension.

To sum up: Our emotional apparatus accepts patterns of stimuli at their face value. If it appears to be a fight that is taking place before us, then, so far as our emotions are concerned, it is a fight. With more data available, our intellect associates the present pattern of stimuli with our past experience of a similar nature so that it reaches an insight that more accurately approaches the truth.

Our intellect may confirm our first impression that a fight is taking place, or it may deduce that it is just the frolicking of some youths, or that it is some other activity of a peaceful nature.

Our emotions serve to get activity quickly under way in an emergency, but they are not too reliable in their appraisal of the true situation.

The flier who knows what to do, who anticipates emergencies and has a plan for handling them, is not likely to yield to fear. However, the emotion takes over in the absence of cerebral direction.

There is also the situation wherein we are unable to solve a problem because we are unable to recognize the problem. We may be unable to recognize the cause of our fear or may be so confused by the sudden impact of stimuli that we cannot think clearly.

If I hear an explosion behind my back, I am likely to show some signs of fear. The explosion may present no actual threat to my security; it may be only a small boy with a cap pistol. Had he fired the pistol from a point where I saw him, I would have experienced no fear. In the case of the student who froze to the controls, when he pushed the control stick forward and the bottom of everything dropped out from under him, when his heart and all his organs seemed to rise into his throat, he was obsessed with a blind, unreasoning fear. In his case, the surprise element was his undoing.

If I had explained to him beforehand that this would happen if he pushed the stick forward too rapidly, he might have seen the whole picture and realized that, while the sensations were unpleasant, there was no serious threat to his safety.

When the airplane reached its terminal velocity and these sensations diminished, he began to see the whole picture and his fear diminished.

It is just as important to demonstrate the sensations the student will experience as a result of certain acts—such as shoving the stick forward violently—as it is to demonstrate for him the effect the same act will have on the attitude of the airplane. The student must learn to control his own attitude as well as the attitude of the airplane.

During the remainder of his course this student who had frozen to the controls was handled with great care. He learned rapidly. Soon he was ready for solo. I hesitated because, somehow, I did not fully trust him.

I noticed that he boasted to his fellow students a great deal. He bragged that he almost went to sleep while flying. Flying was so simple that it was boring. He surely showed no more signs of fear. At that time, I was too naive to realize that he was masking his fears.

At last I could put off his solo no longer. He was doing a good job of flying. Came the day, I climbed out of the old Jenny, slapped him on the back, and said, "She's all yours. Good luck!"

Little did I realize how badly he would need some luck. With some misgivings I watched the old Jenny weave down the field and stagger into the air. However, the student made a nice flight around the airport and came in judging his approach nicely. I saw with relief that he would land well within the boundaries of the airport. But some fifty feet above the ground he threw his hands above his head. The airplane dived into the ground, turned over on its back, and slithered along, disintegrating into small pieces . . . my chickens had come home to roost.

As I raced across the melting snow to pull his body from the wreckage, the thought insistently hammered through my brain, "He's dead and I'm responsible!"

In that moment of anguish it took no reasoning, no analytic tracing of events, to see clearly where this catastrophe had had its beginning. In one illuminating flash I saw the whole chain of events that had led to this tragic mess.

On that first flight I had allowed him to stumble into a situation for which he was unprepared, with which he was utterly unable to cope. In that moment of terror, he had received a deep psychic wound—a wound that never healed.

Yet it could have been healed save for my own blind lack of understanding. This student was an extremely sensitive young man. He despised himself for what he believed to have been a cowardly performance. He had covered the wound to hide it from his fellow students and from me. He had masked his fears. Yes, he had fooled me. But never for one minute had he fooled himself.

When I had climbed out of the plane to turn it over to him for his first solo, I had noticed him trembling a little— with eagerness, I thought. That lousy take-off, so different from his others ... he was fighting for control.

The fear that he had so carefully covered was an open wound now. He felt inadequate. Fear was mounting—fear that he would muff the landing. He fought against it but to no avail. His trembling feet beat a tattoo on the rudder bar. Tension mounted higher and higher; something had to give. Something did give when the plane was but fifty feet from the ground.

With success but a few seconds away, he'd said, "I just can't do it!" And throwing his hands above his head he gave up. He relieved the tension by total surrender.

Fortunately, the young man escaped injury. For the first time in my life I washed out a student, not because he had destroyed an airplane I could ill afford to lose, but because I believed he never would be safe at the controls.

The incident left me with a scar too. I found myself riding with students long after I knew they were ready to solo. I came to dread that moment when I must climb out, gaily slap a student on the back, and exclaim, "OK! She's all yours. Good luck!"

That is why I become interested in learning why pilots behave as they do in various emergencies. In the years that have followed, as I accumulated more than 10,000 hours in the air, I became greatly interested in cases where pilots miraculously escaped disaster by superior flying. I have studied records to try to determine in each case what made the pilot behave so well.

The most dramatic examples, however, are those that end in disaster. In these cases I ask myself, "What would I have done had I been sitting in his place?"

The most uncertain element in flying today is the pilot. Airplanes are carefully engineered; we know what to expect of them. We know what they will do. But when we can predict equally well what pilots will do, aviation will be much safer.

# 2

# Adapting to the New Environment

I asked an army flying instructor, "Doesn't it make you feel a little mean to wash out a student who has tried desperately hard to make the grade?"

"Hell, no!" he replied. "I just imagine myself flying next to him in a night formation."

This is the justification for the relatively hard-boiled training methods prevalent in the military service. The lives of good men and the success of an engagement depend upon the behavior of other men. Those unfitted for flying must be weeded out during the training period, which must serve two purposes. It must prepare men for adaptation to a new environment and it must weed out those who cannot successfully adapt. Men are even more expendable in training than in battle.

That is why nearly 4,000,000 men were rejected as unfit for military service during World War II. At times the records showed that men were being discharged for psychological reasons alone faster than new men were being inducted.

Probably the majority of the men rejected could have been made into excellent soldiers by the application of these psychological principles in their training if time had permitted and if there had been a sufficient number of men available from not only those who understood these principles but as well as from those that govern military operations.

Not only do some men possess greater adaptive ability than others, but for some the change from the peacetime to the military environment requires less adaptation.

Take the case of Mr. Squeamish. Mr. Squeamish was an

only child. He had been reared in a genteel atmosphere. After his graduation from Harvard he'd gone in for designing women's clothing—and quite successfully, too.

His friends were cultivated gentlefolk like himself. He had never been called upon to defend himself physically. The idea of taking the life of a fellow human was distasteful in the extreme.

All his life he had slept in a room by himself and bathed in private. It is doubtful if anyone had seen his nude body since the time his mother had adjusted his last diaper. Mr. S. prized his privacy.

Then war breaks out and he receives the customary "Greetings" from the President of the United States. Mr. Squeamish exchanges his expensively tailored suit for the uniform of the United States Army.

How will he adjust to this new life into which he is being inducted? How will he like sleeping, dressing, and bathing in a room with a hundred other men? Not a moment of privacy will be his. How will he adjust to the hundred-and-one details of military life that are so different from the life to which he has been accustomed?

The army will throw the book at him. Some day a brutal enemy will give Mr. Squeamish the works. From the beginning he might as well get used to taking it. If he can't take it, now is the time to find it out.

For the other extreme, let's take a look at Joe Dukes. Joe grew up in a large family. He slept in a small room with four brothers and two sisters. He swam in a muddy hole down by the railroad bridge, clad in nature's garments. He sold newspapers and fought for his rights with a tough neighborhood gang. His father was a severe taskmaster who taught Joe to obey.

Assuming that both Mr. Squeamish and Joe Dukes possess ability to adapt, who will adapt the more readily to the military environment?

There are flying instructors who pride themselves on being hard-boiled. For the first flight, they will strap the student securely into his seat and say, "Hang on, son. We're going for a ride." Then they will take the beginner up and literally wring him out. They will start him flying in rough, gusty weather. "Might as well get used to it," they will say. "You've got to learn to take the rough with the smooth."

Of course, many students come through such hard-boiled courses of instruction with flying colors. They make the grade easily; they are the "naturals." Since childhood, they have engaged in outdoor sports of all kinds, driven motor cars, motorcycles, speed boats, and other mechanical contrivances. They are at home on a horse or in a sailboat. They have a multitude of reflexes that require but little change to adapt them to this new environment. Yet even these "naturals" would make far better pilots if given a sensible step-by-step course of instruction.

The man who does not bring such a well-developed background of conditioned reflexes to the flying field will naturally learn more slowly—but he can learn, and often he makes an excellent pilot. In a way, flying offers him more than it does the "natural." It fills more of a need in his life. Yet, if he is not properly handled, he may fail to adapt to flying.

We cannot find a finer example of adaptation than that offered by the child. All of us must go through a similar process when we adapt to any new environment.

When a baby leaves the protection of its mother's womb and enters the world, it is entering a new environment to which it must learn to adapt itself if it is going to survive.

When a child encounters a situation that he cannot possibly understand or cope with, a situation so utterly baffling that the child is terror-stricken, the incident may leave psychic impressions that will mark that child for life, conditioning his outlook on life, his emotions, and influencing his decisions.

In the protective environment of the home, the child usually meets the problems of his environment in easy, controlled stages. In this manner he gains strength much as one gains immunity from disease through vaccination. But if that child is overly protected and shielded from the vicissitudes of life in these formative years, he may never learn to adapt himself to them in its later years. He may go through his entire life dependent upon others.

If the child meets life with insufficient protection from the home, his confidence may be weakened and he may go through life with secret fears that persist, regardless of how carefully he may mask them from his fellows.

The ideal home is one in which a proper balance is sought. The child is prepared for the problems of life by meeting them in easy stages under the controlled conditions of the home environment. With the guidance afforded him, he learns to adjust in a confident manner to this new and changing environment in which he is to live.

The flying student is in much the same situation as the child, in that he is entering a new environment to which he will adapt with ease and confidence if these fundamental principles are observed in his training.

The capable instructor is far more than a safety pilot to save the student and equipment from mishap. His duty does not end when he has demonstrated to the student the proper pressures he must apply to the controls to produce the desired response from the airplane.

He must plan the student's flying experience so that he will learn in easy, controlled steps. He must always present a minor situation first and work up to the more difficult situation.

It is as foolhardy to start a student out in rough, gusty air as it would be to teach a child his first steps in walking in the traffic of a busy downtown street.

The instructor must train the student to succeed—not to fail. The student must learn to master difficult situations, but he learns through first mastering simpler situations.

Here is an example: In teaching a student to make forced landings the capable instructor will first start with a power-off landing in which the motor is cut in such a position that the student can hardly fail to land on the airport. Then the instructor will proceed to more difficult problems, until the student can make a forced landing into the airport from almost any conceivable position, when the motor is cut.

The instructor will then take the student near some large field and again cut the motor; thereafter practice will be switched to smaller fields. The instructor shows the student how to pick a suitable emergency landing field and then begins cutting the motor at points where the student must learn to use some judgment in the selection of the field as well as skill to maneuver the airplane into the field. In this manner the student will learn by such easy steps that his confidence grows as he acquires the necessary flying skills.

Some hard-boiled instructors, however, begin by taking a student out over rough country, where the only available fields are small, irregular, and rough. Then without warning, they cut the motor and shout, "Forced landing! Let's see you pick out a field and get into it." Barring an act of God or some miracle of luck, the student fails. Then the hard-boiled instructor asks, "What would happen if the motor should cut in a place like this when I'm not along?"

This is an ideal manner for conditioning a pilot whose heart will skip a beat any time the motor sputters for as long as he flies. This is the way to develop a pilot who will have a morbid fear of forced landings. Because he is afraid, he is less likely to develop the necessary skill. If he does, it will not benefit him to the fullest because of his lack of confidence. His fear will add to the element of fatigue when he flies cross-country. If you want him to become a poor pilot and end up some day by breaking his neck, this is the way a student should be trained.

The one great fundamental fact that every flying instructor should understand is: A student should never be placed in a situation that is impossible for him to master; he must be prepared for the difficult situation through mastering simpler situations that lead up to the difficult situation.

Many instructors like to impress students with the gravity

of certain situations in the belief that it will spur them on to becoming more proficient in learning to master the situation. They overlook the possibility that, when a problem seems too difficult, we may simply give up and direct our attention to evading the situation, instead of attempting to master it. This is exactly what many psychoneurotics did in military life.

My first student impressed these facts on my mind. The day following his enrollment I had a long cross-country flight to make. I decided to take him along on the trip. What a trip it turned out to be! We flew through a severe storm. We got lost. Motor trouble forced us to land. I had a feeling that our safe return may have been directed by the guiding hand of an ever-watchful Providence.

The following day, this student's landlady said to me, "You better have a talk with that Clarence. He's mighty low in his mind. Says he's never going home. Talked this flying so much that he can't bear to have 'em find out that he couldn't make it."

I found Clarence had indeed made up his mind that flying was beyond his capabilities. He said mournfully, "I could never do the things you had to do on that trip."

"There was a time when I couldn't do them either," I said. "In fact, I was very unhappy myself during much of that trip. It was hardly a fair sample of flying."

I pointed to a mountain in the distance. "You couldn't possibly get to that mountain in one long step. But, if you want to get there badly enough, all you have to do is to start walking. You can get there by taking one step at a time— and that is the way you are going to learn to fly. It isn't going to be difficult because it is going to be divided into a lot of steps. And it will be easy for you to master each step. All it takes is a little patience and determination. The question is: Do you want to get to that mountain badly enough to have the patience to make all the steps necessary to take you there?"

Clarence developed into a mighty fine pilot.

There is scarcely a problem in life that you and I cannot

solve, just as Clarence solved his problem, by breaking that problem down into easy steps. And then taking one step at a time till we get there. When we try to make it in one giant stride, the problem may seem impossible. We fail if we try to take steps that are too long for us.

It is never a question of, Can I reach the mountain? It is always a question of, Does it mean enough to me to reach it? Do I want to get to that mountain so much that I have the determination and the patience to take each step in turn until I get there?

Some problems may not seem to adapt themselves to a division of steps, but the solution is much the same. We attack them as we would eat an apple, taking a bite at a time around the circumference, approaching the problem from every angle. No matter how large the apple may be, if we keep taking one bite at a time we will eventually reach the core.

When entering a new environment we find that certain features of this new environment are greatly different from our previous environment. Usually it is these new features that disturb us the most.

The most disturbing factors in the flying environment are:

(1) Frequency of acceleration and deceleration, and sudden changes in direction of motion.

(2) The fact that this new environment is a dynamic state in which survival depends upon a continuous course of progressive motion, a state in which we can neither stop nor back up.

Those who have never flown may be surprised that I have not included a feeling of insecurity because of altitude, but one of the most pleasing phenomena of flight is the absence of any feeling of insecurity because of height. A person who feels giddy and nauseated when standing atop an ordinary stepladder will be perfectly at ease two miles above the earth in an airplane.

The flier has temporarily severed his connection with the earth and is in a new environment. He is in a world of its own—

the airplane. So long as the airplane is functioning perfectly he has no feeling of insecurity. Sometimes in making a turn around a pylon, one aligns the wing of the airplane with the pylon so that the pylon appears as an extension of the airplane wing, linking the airplane to the earth. At such a moment, the pilot may experience a feeling of insecurity and giddiness the same as though he were looking down from the top of a tall building.

Because of this indifference to height, we find that most flying enthusiasts maintain that there is nothing disturbing about this new environment. In the pages that follow we shall see how wrong they are.

It is true that man experiences changes in the direction of motion and in acceleration and deceleration in his earth-bound environment, though usually of a less frequent occurrence and of a less severe degree. He understands, however, the significance of these changes when they occur in his earthbound environment more readily than he understands the significance of the same changes in his flying environment. By comparison with near-by objects on the ground he can see at a glance whether such changes will endanger him.

In the air he has no near-by objects with which to interpret the meaning of these changes. And the meaning of the changes is often still further confused because the labyrinthine canals in his ears sometimes convey sensations to the brain that differ from those perceived by the eyes. Changes he does not understand are likely to disturb him.

For instance, you can walk through a warehouse in broad daylight hearing a medley of sounds that do not alarm you in the least, because you can see at a glance that these noises offer no threat to your security. But try walking through this same warehouse at midnight when it is pitch dark, listening to the same noises. The slightest creak of a timber in an overhead truss may start your heart hammering furiously and the hair to stand erect on the back of your neck. Now you are not so sure that these noises do not offer some threat to your security. In fact, you may rather easily convince yourself that some terrifying peril is stalking your steps. Turn on a light, however, and you will find your fears subsiding. The unknowns, the things we do not understand, cause our greatest fears.

In the same manner, these sensations of motion you do not so fully understand may alarm you more in the air than the same motions would alarm you in your earthbound environment. They alarm you less as you come to understand and to anticipate them.

Rather quickly, the passenger adapts himself to flying because he is a spectator rather than an actor. He views these changes in a detached manner because he knows it is not his problem to react to them. He leaves that to the pilot who is getting paid for it.

Of course, the situation is a little different if the passenger has no confidence in the pilot; then he may be doing some mental back-seat driving.

It is a far different situation when one first takes the controls of an airplane with the purpose of guiding its flight. Now all of these changes of motion, acceleration, and deceleration become significant. The pilot must react to them intelligently if he is to control the airplane.

He pushes the stick forward, and the airplane starts rapidly downward. No longer does he regard this change in the detached manner with which he might have regarded it as a passenger. Until he can interpret its significance, and until he knows what action to take, the emotion of fear will snowball to great proportions.

The capable instructor does not allow the student to wander about and frighten himself in the darkness of the warehouse; he keeps the light on by helping the student to understand and to anticipate events.

Before having the student attempt a movement of the controls or a maneuver, the wise instructor first performs the movement or maneuver himself, with the student following through on the controls. By this procedure the student is spared none of the problems of flight but he is not allowed to encounter these problems until he understands them and is capable of dealing with them. He learns in an easy, confident manner to adapt successfully to the disturbing factors in this new environment.

At a more advanced stage the student becomes aware of the second disturbing factor in this new environment: the necessity of continuous progressive movement.

In his earthbound existence he can stop to think. In the air he must learn to think while in motion for if the airplane is allowed to stop it will corkscrew down and make a big hole in the ground. Thinking while in motion presents the disadvantage that by the time you reach your conclusion the situation has changed and you must modify your conclusion to conform to the new situation.

The flier who gets lost must keep right on flying while he orients himself. While he is examining the map to determine his location he is moving away from that exact location; once he has spotted his position he is no longer there. Quickly he must estimate his present position from a comparison with the newly established check-point. Not only must the student-pilot strive to avoid getting lost in the first place but he must learn some system whereby he can quickly determine his position once he is lost.

How different this is from his earthbound environment where, walking along strange streets in a busy city, the pedestrian can stop and examine a street map of the city, or read street signs, or ask some passer-by for directions, and leisurely decide where he is. Down on the street he can make plans for getting back on course in a leisurely manner.

Likewise, when he motors down a highway and his motor suddenly stops the driver can pull off to the side of the road. He can take plenty of time to figure out what is wrong and to decide what action he will take.

However, when motor trouble develops in the air the pilot has only a limited amount of time to plan and decide. Every moment he wastes may be carrying him nearer to disaster.

Hence, he must at all times have in his mind a well-formulated procedure for such an occasion.

When he finds himself plunging into a storm he cannot stop to think it over. He must turn back at once or he will soon find himself in the center of the storm. He must know how to judge storms, he must know the wisest course to take when he encounters one, and he must keep one step ahead of weather developments.

Always he is harassed by this paucity of time. To compensate for this, he must plan in advance for every possible kind of an emergency, since there is so little time to plan when the emergency occurs.

These factors may give him a feeling of insecurity, comparable to that suffered by the victim of claustrophobia. In his case he is harassed by a lack of time rather than a lack of space.

The victim of claustrophobia seldom suffers from any actual lack of space; the pilot who has learned what to do in the various emergencies seldom suffers from any real lack of time in which to perform his duties. In both cases, an emotional feeling of insufficiency is what disturbs the victim; one feels cramped for lack of space in which to act, and the other feels cramped for a lack of time in which to act effectively.

Feeling a lack of time, the pilot hurries his actions, with his attention on future problems instead of on the problem at hand, until finally he finds himself in the very position he so greatly fears.

This feeling—that something can happen which will place him in a situation in which he will not have sufficient time to plan and act—is one of the most harassing fears that can nag a pilot. But he can obtain peace of mind by preparing for any contingency and by thoroughly planning each flight, making sure that no detail is overlooked.

No one can go through life without encountering an occasional emergency. As a nation we can never be sure that some other nation will not suddenly attack us. However, if we are prepared to repel such an attack, we can still enjoy peace of mind.

The pilot who will not make the effort to acquaint himself with all the emergencies that can occur and plan a course of action for every possible emergency pays a fearful price in peace of mind. All during the flight the pilot who takes off without a map, or without planning his course, or without checking the weather, or without making sure that he has sufficient fuel, will be nagged by anxiety.

Worst of all, this sort of thing has a progressively cumulating possibility for disaster. The careless pilot is continually hurrying for fear he will get caught short. In his hurrying, he shorts himself by failing to take all due precautions to insure his safety. Then he worries while he flies and thus cannot give his full attention to the problems at hand.

Herein lies the factor that so often enables the slow learner to become a far more capable pilot than some "naturals." He learns to divide each problem into steps and masters each step. From this he learns to anticipate future problems and makes a step-by-step plan for their solution. When he encounters trouble, he has a plan for action already prepared and keeps his mind on each step in turn as he masters the situation. Since he has learned to master problems in this step-by-step fashion, he is not likely to leave out any important step. He prepares thoroughly for each flight.

Many "naturals" learn so easily that they have little reason for breaking their problems down into steps. In one great leap they seem able to deal with the whole problem. They plan for future emergencies in the same general way. They have no definite step-by-step procedure in mind and, when preparing for a flight, often overlook important details.

No student need feel bad because he is a slow learner. If he capitalizes on it, this very factor may cause him to become a superior type of pilot.

# 3

# Why We Get Off the Beam

As Hermann Goering saw his beloved Luftwaffe dwindling, its strength taxed by heavy losses, he made the petulant remark, "We suffer these heavy losses because the German pilot has an incurable mania for wanting to sleep in his own bed."

Goering was lamenting the fact that pilots passed over airfields where they might have safely landed, even though their planes had been damaged by enemy action, because of an insane desire to get back to their own base. He was disturbed by the fact that his Eager Beavers who were fanatically determined to do a superior job were the very ones that met with disaster.

Flying instructors frequently ask in exasperation: "Why is it that students who just don't give a damn take to flying like a duck takes to water, while students who try the hardest so often fail?"

You also may have wondered why you sometimes fumble and stumble your way through situations where success means so much to you. You may have asked yourself, "Why do I suffer from buck-fever and checkitis? Why do I do my worst when I want to do my best? Why do I so often fail under pressure?"

Watch the individual players in a football game, a baseball game, or in any sport. You will notice that the winning players are those individuals who perform best when under pressure, when the game is at stake.

Men who are successful in business or in any other human endeavor are those who perform well under pressure. That is one reason why the person with mediocre talent and ability so often outstrips those with far greater talents and far greater ability.

Why don't we all perform at our best in these critical situations?

The answer is extremely simple, but to apply this simple truth is not so simple.

You may have noticed that wild animals almost invariably put on a superb performance when in a critical situation, in their native habitat. In the wild animal, as in you and me, the sympathetic emotions marshal the strength of the body and initiate reflex activities that are characteristic of the emotion involved. Is it any wonder that the animal puts forth a first-rate performance?

Since the native habitat of the wild animal has changed but little, the reflex activities initiated by the emotions of the animal have not become obsolete. Our own environment, our native habitat, is subject to such enormous and rapid change that the reflex activities initiated by our emotions do not always fit the present circumstances. Instead, many of our outdated, obsolete emotional responses often cause us to defeat ourselves through our own efforts.

You and I, however, can recondition these emotional responses so that they will again fit the situation that arouses the emotion. We can learn to recognize those situations wherein our emotional responses are so likely to defeat us or lead to ineffective action.

When a person who sincerely desires to succeed defeats himself through his own frantic efforts, it is a heartbreaking experience. Certainly sincere effort should not become a factor contributing to defeat. And sincere effort never will contribute to any man's defeat, if he is on the beam headed in the proper direction.

Suppose we are making a cross-country flight, using an obsolete map upon which many of the names of the indicated towns and cities are no longer correct. We might compare this inaccurate map to a chart of our motivations wherein our emotions direct us toward false goals. Just as the inaccurate map might head us toward the wrong city, our emotions may often trick us into selecting false, unimportant goals.

You are familiar with the device that soldiers use to draw enemy fire, wherein a helmet or some other object is poked enticingly into view. Wasting ammunition on such an unimportant target is similar to the way we waste our energy in fruitless effort when we select unimportant goals.

Goering's pilots wanted to get their aircraft safely on the ground in friendly territory after completing a mission. Instead, they allowed their emotions to egg them on to their own base with a faltering motor, passing over airports where they might have landed safely. An unimportant goal lured them away from their real goal. In our simplest acts we often fail because we place so much emphasis on the wrong motivation.

The practical value of psychology lies in the fact that it can teach us to recognize those false goals. Often, such knowledge can enable us to perform a difficult task with ease, simply because we avoid wasting our efforts on the false goals and on unimportant minor goals.

Some unscrupulous individuals use their knowledge of psychology to trick their fellowman into selecting a goal that will not benefit that man but will benefit the unscrupulous individual. The wily politician may use his knowledge of psychology to trick the voter into voting to his own disadvantage, but to the benefit of the wily politician. A cunning salesman or an unscrupulous advertising executive may use his knowledge of psychology to trick people into buying worthless merchandise or goods that are of no benefit to them. In like manner you and I may allow our emotions to trick us into selecting goals that do not lead us to the things we really want.

It seems obvious that, if you and I can use our knowledge of psychology to influence other people, we should also be able to use such knowledge to influence our own lives. To accomplish this end, we must understand our emotions.

Emotions are important. Our sympathetic emotions energize our nervous system. Have you ever examined an old

35

alternating-current generator that depends upon a small auxiliary dynamo to energize the field windings of the larger generator? This huge generator will not generate current until its field windings are excited by the current from the small auxiliary dynamo.

This is a fair analogy to the manner in which our emotions marshal both our mental and our physical resources for action and cause us to work at an accelerated speed. Our emotions also initiate certain reflex activities that are characteristic of the emotion that is involved. This includes reflex activity in the cerebral cortex as well as our physical reflexes.

Both our emotional responses and our intellectual responses are learned from experience but with this difference: most of our emotional learning develops from firsthand experience, from the things that happen directly to us, whereas we can learn, intellectually, by making associations from direct experience, from recalled experience, from the experience of our fellows, and even from the accumulated experience of all mankind—from all the experience that has been set down from the day that man learned to write to the present moment.

If a bell is rung each time a dog is fed, the dog will eventually become conditioned to the ringing of the bell to the extent that it will react to the ringing of the bell much as it reacts to the sight of food, because it has learned to expect food to accompany the ringing of the bell. In much the same manner, you and I learn that a ten-dollar bill may be exchanged for groceries, so that a ten-dollar bill in our pocket gives us much the same feeling of security from hunger as would a pantry full of groceries.

That is how we learn emotionally.

The higher centers of the brain enable us to learn to make more specialized responses to stimuli through using a wider variety of associations from the richer field of data that are available to the intellect.

We can make intellectual associations from direct

36

experience, we can recall our past experiences and assemble them in a variety of associations and project them into the future, and we can make associations from the experience of our fellows and from the great mass of experience accumulated through several thousand years. Through the use of this great mass of data, our intellect can make forecasts that are far more accurate than our emotional feelings.

Emotionally, we may feel that a dictatorship is a suitable goal, because the one dictator with whom we have had firsthand experience was a benevolent dictator under whose rule we were exceedingly prosperous and happy.

Intellectually, with a wider range of data with which to make a wide range of associations, we will compare this benevolent dictator with other dictators who have caused unhappiness and have left ruin in their wake. After making such comparisons we are more likely to select a worth-while goal.

Through our intellect, we break a problem down into steps that we can master. Then we solve the problem through a procedure in which we solve each step in its proper sequence. Hence, our intellectual response is not directed towards the ultimate end but is directed to the step at hand, the step by means of which we finally reach our ultimate goal.

A common mistake that leads to ineffective action is to direct our attention to the end, to our final goal, instead of to the step at hand which is our immediate goal and for the moment is the only goal that is of any importance to us.

When a flying student worries about his rate of progress, when he worries about the respect with which he is regarded by his instructor and his fellow students, or about his chances of passing a flight check, he is making this mistake of directing his attention to a goal that can only be reached by first solving the problem at hand; the mistake is as ridiculous as trying to jump to your apartment on the sixth floor instead of using the stairs.

Suppose you are flying from St. Louis to Chicago. You tune in on the first radio range station en route as you leave St. Louis and direct your attention to reaching this first range station. After reaching the first radio range station you tune in on the next range station on your route, and continue this procedure until you eventually reach Chicago.

If you were navigating by pilotage, you would select check points at regular intervals along your route and would head toward each one in turn. No one but a fool would strain his eyes in a fruitless effort to see Chicago as he climbed out of Lambert Field in St. Louis. Instead he would direct his attention to his first check point.

Yet, in the simplest problems in life, instead of directing our attention to the step at hand, we often direct our attention to a goal that can only be reached by first solving the step at hand. Is it any wonder that we so often fail?

Our emotions are always aroused in the critical situations in life when we are the most determined to make our action effective. Oftentimes these emotions lead us to defeat through unintelligent effort.

How can you and I avoid allowing our emotions to trick us into selecting unimportant goals? In the same manner that we avoid being influenced by the tricky salesman or the wily politician: by learning to distinguish between a purely emotional appeal or incentive and an intellectual appeal or incentive, and through becoming exceedingly cautious and wary in situations where emotional appeals can so easily lead us astray.

We can even reduce our procedure to a simple formula.

1.  Will this goal really benefit us?

2.  Can this goal be reached without first reaching some other goal? If not, the means by which we are to reach our final goal is the goal toward which we must first direct our efforts.

Since our emotions provide us with extra power and strength in critical moments, by marshaling our resources for action, our problem is to direct this power and strength, summoned by our emotions, into effective action that is directed by our intellect.

You can remember when it was a common practice for

tough, two-fisted foremen to curse the men working under them when the task those men were performing required great application of strength. A group of angry men could lift a steel rail that could not have been budged by the same group when their emotions were not aroused.

In such a situation, the emotion of anger aroused by the cursing of the foreman mobilized the resources of power and strength required for effective action. This strength might have been directed to punching the foreman's nose had he not been a man to discourage the selection of such a goal; or the energy might merely have caused the men to smolder mentally. But the good workman seemed to understand the factors involved; at any rate, he directed the strength that had been marshaled by his anger to the task at hand.

You and I can make the same choice. We can direct the strength summoned by our emotions into constructive effort, or we can allow it to be wasted on unimportant goals.

I knew a wealthy man who designed and built a novel airplane motor. When he had it finished and running he was so displeased with his motor that he became angry and, picking up a sledge-hammer, he smashed all that he had labored so long to build. After a couple of weeks he would set to work rebuilding the motor, only to end up by smashing it again in another fit of anger.

He could have used this power and strength, summoned by his frustration, to drive him forward to seek an answer to his problem. Emotional tension often reaches a point where it becomes extremely unpleasant, but the power, the strength, and the energy that emotion marshals may serve to drive us forward to success, if properly directed.

A man coming at you with a knife may arouse the emotion of fear within you, but, if you know what to do, how to do it, and go into action to do it, the emotion of fear may not reach extreme proportions.

Suppose something blocks action—perhaps you do not know how to act, perhaps there is a mental conflict as to which of several available courses of action you should adopt, or perhaps you do not possess either the physical capacity or the mental capacity to carry out the action successfully.

It is as though you had built a dam across a stream. This power for action begins to build up as water builds up behind the dam. Your emotions mount as the water mounts behind the dam, until finally either the dam bursts or the water flows over the dam. In you all this power and strength that has been building up finally surges into action, either physical or mental. Mental action may take the form of breaking the problem down into easy steps thus by-passing the dam, or mental action may take the form of an escape or defense mechanism, a purely imaginary solution of the problem.

The unknown arouses great fears; action is blocked, since we cannot act when we do not know what it is about the situation that seems to threaten our security. But mental action is possible; the unknown may arouse the exploratory emotion, the emotion of curiosity, which causes us to seek to discover what features of the situation seem to threaten our security and why. When we seek to learn more about the situation, curiosity is likely to become the dominant emotion rather than fear.

Our intellect tends to inhibit our emotional responses, but when action is blocked our emotions will build behind the dam that is blocking action until an emotional response may be forced upon us, unless our intellect can come up with a mental solution before the emotional tension gets out of bounds.

That is why we plan for emergencies in advance. That is why we plan our future actions, so that we may have a solution clearly in mind, ready to be put into action when the emergency arises. If we have this plan worked out so well that it is clear in our mind, we act decisively, our action being directed from our intellect. If we have no plan for action, or if the plan is hazy, we may act hesitantly or allow our emotions to direct our action.

There may be times when the very speed of the emotional response may save our life, as in an instance when such a response is a wild leap to escape a truck that is roaring down upon us.

Many of our emotional responses have become outdated. Where they once served to enable us to adjust to our environment, they may now hinder us, because our environment has changed so rapidly that they are obsolete.

Where the emotional response is not obsolete, where it leads us toward an important goal, it is to be preferred to the intellectual response because it starts us quickly into action, and in some critical situations that demand quick action the speed of the emotional response may serve to make action effective even to the point of saving our lives.

Fortunately, we can recondition some of our obsolete emotional responses, bringing them up to date. We will examine a familiar situation for which the airplane pilot must recondition an obsolete emotional response.

You are taking off. You must clear a brick wall fifty feet high at the end of the runway. Anxious to clear the wall, you have climbed too steeply. The airplane quivers and the nose settles. Your obsolete emotions would cause you to yank the controls back to force the airplane up into the air and over the wall.

In this critical moment that demands split-second action, an intellectual response might come too late. To sit and do nothing may be nearly as disastrous as yielding to the obsolete emotion.

At this point, thorough training may save your life if, during your training, you have reconditioned the obsolete emotional response that would cause you to yank the stick back when the nose begins to settle in a stall. Your new response to that quiver, coupled with the settling of the nose, is automatically to ease the stick ahead to regain flying speed before resuming your climb to clear the wall.

There are instructors who fail to recondition thoroughly some of these obsolete emotional responses, and the students trained by such instructors very often stall and crash in just such critical situations.

The Civil Aeronautics Authority reports that even today more than half of our aviation fatalities are the result of the stall-and-spin type of accident.

It is not enough to know that the nose must be lowered to regain flying speed when an airplane stalls; the emotional response must be reconditioned to the point where the pilot will automatically, without hesitation, ease forward on the controls as the airplane approaches a stalled condition.

To sum up: The goals we select direct our actions.

If we are not wary, the emotions that mobilize our resources of power and strength to make action effective may also direct that action toward false or unimportant goals.

Our purpose in this study is to learn to direct this power and strength to the really important goals, so that this great force may jet-propel us to success.

We have available two methods for accomplishing this feat:

1. For those critical situations that demand split-second action, we recondition our emotional response so that we make the desired response to stimuli without thought.

This method demands that we practice until we automatically make the correct response without hesitation when we encounter a situation that demands such a response. It is important to point out that it is not enough to know the correct procedure to meet such situations effectively; we must be trained or must train ourselves to make the correct response automatically.

2. For those situations that do not demand swift action, we plan a procedure. To be effective this method demands that we thoroughly understand and have clearly in mind each and every step of the procedure.

If the procedure is not clear in our mind, if there is any doubt or confusion, we are likely to act hesitantly or we may even react to some obsolete emotional response instead of putting the planned procedure into action.

In a great many cases, the individual who fumbles and

hesitates can trace his hesitation and awkward fumbling to insufficient preparation, to the fact that the procedure is a little hazy in his mind. He thinks that he knows the procedure, but he lacks the absolute, certain, positive knowledge that leads to clean-cut, decisive action.

During World War II pilots in the Air Transport Command were often trained to fly a dozen or more types of military aircraft, including twin-engine and four-engine bombers. They were compelled to learn a tremendous amount of procedure that included special emergency procedures to be adopted when some part of the airplane such as a landing gear, a motor, or a propeller failed to operate properly. After learning the procedures for a new type of aircraft, they were checked out on the airplane by transition instructors.

Many of these pilots had thousands of hours in the air, yet they muddled through transition in an unsatisfactory manner. It was common for such pilots to blame their fumbling upon checkitis, and such a diagnosis was often well founded, but, in most cases, it was demonstrated that at least part of their trouble was the fact that they did not really have the procedure clear in their minds.

The Army tried a new plan; after studying the procedures for the airplane, the pilot was required to take an examination on the subject before he was eligible for transition. Transition instructors reported that the situation improved as a result of these examinations. They also discovered that, other things being equal, those pilots who made good grades on a quickly written examination performed with clean-cut, decisive action during transition.

It is, of course, understood that we may at times find it advisable to modify our planned procedure to adapt it to a special situation.

We might liken the energy marshaled by our emotions to the energy released by the splitting of the atom; either can be used constructively to make life richer and fuller, or either may be used to destroy ourselves—the choice lies with us.

43

# 4

# The Case of the Absent-minded Pilot

Jake was a chemical engineer and a good one. He possessed a sharp mind. I chuckle when I recall an incident that occurred on his fourth training flight.

I turned to Jake and said, "OK, you taxi down to the far corner of the field, then we'll take off into the wind."

As we reached the far corner of the field I said, "Jake, you've been doing good work. I'm going to let you make the take-off today. Take it easy and if you get into any trouble I'll take over."

Nothing happened. Finally I turned around and asked, "What are you waiting for?"

"I don't know," he replied, "but something seems to be missing. I wish you'd take a look."

I climbed out. Walking back, I looked into his cock-pit. Something surely was missing—the control stick. Someone had carried a passenger in the trainer and, as was customary on such occasions, had removed the student's control stick so that it would not be in the passenger's way.

I tried to put myself in Jake's place, to understand such extreme absent-mindedness.

Most likely he had been deep in some interesting problem in his chemical laboratory when, glancing at the clock, he saw that he was about due at the airport for his flying lesson. In all probability he'd grabbed his hat and dashed out to his car and headed for the airport, but his mind was still on the problem that fascinated him. He drove through a red light, and at the next intersection there was a loud honking of horns from the cars lined up behind him while he sat deep in thought long after the light had turned green.

When he reached the airport, he'd climbed into the airplane with his mind still centered on that problem back in his laboratory. His thoughts were a thousand miles away from flying as he taxied out to take off. No wonder Jake wasn't aware that the control stick was missing, since he had only to use the throttle and rudder while taxiing.

After that I would engage Jake in a little conversation, usually asking him a number of questions relative to the particular problem of the day before we went out to the airplane. I made sure that he had his attention directed to flying before we went up for a lesson.

The man who pursues an intellectual career must be able to hold his attention on the problem at hand. In training himself to do this, he may lose some of the flexibility of directing his attention to new problems. This flexibility is essential to the man of action.

The man of action must learn to direct his attention to the problem at hand and hold it there until that problem is solved. Only then can he switch it to another problem that in its turn becomes the problem at hand.

Suppose you gave me a three-gallon pail full of water and asked me to fill a gallon jug. If I just poured the water out of the pail at the neck of the jug, very little of it would enter the jug, most of it being wasted. However, if I used a funnel I could fill the jug easily and have a couple of gallons of water left over.

It is much the same problem we face in directing our attention to the problem at hand. When our full attention is directed to the problem we solve it easily, with a surplus of energy left over. When we fail to direct our attention, much of our energy is wasted and we are likely to become exhausted and are even more likely to fail to solve the problem.

William James, the great psychologist, has pointed out that most of us fail to use more than twenty per cent of our capabilities for success. The successful men are those who use more than twenty per cent of their capabilities through directing their attention instead of allowing it to scatter. They don't waste their energy on trivial details and false goals. These successful men use a funnel to fill the jug.

Suppose you are going to make a non-stop airplane flight from New York to Paris. You know that you have sufficient fuel to complete the flight, with a slight reserve. After taking off from La Guardia Airport, before heading out to sea, you decide to fly over and wave good-by to a pretty blonde who works in a cigar factory at Lancaster, Pa.

Then you head out to sea and, after settling down to the monotonous grind, you notice a small iceberg floating in the water below you and decide that it would be fun to circle north of your course to see how big those icebergs really are before being melted down by warmer waters.

On course again, your curiosity about the icebergs satisfied, you suddenly notice smoke on the horizon far to the south and fly down, circle the ocean liner and maybe give it a buzz-job.

So—when you find yourself sitting in your little rubber life-raft, tossed upon the white-frothed waves of the North Atlantic, you say to yourself, "I shouldn't have tried to make this damn flight—it just can't be done—these airplanes don't carry enough gasoline for such a trip."

Preposterous! Sure it's preposterous. Neither you nor I would be so asinine. We would head directly out to sea in a bee-line for Paris the moment we left La Guardia Airport, holding a steady course until we reached our goal. No side attraction could possibly tempt us off our course for a single minute.

It is unfortunate that we do not take such an attitude toward all of our problems.

Flying students often compare their progress with the progress made by fellow students. They worry about what their instructor is thinking of them. They try to estimate whether they are making normal progress. They become overanxious to solo.

47

While engaged in solving one problem, their attention is on some other problem. The funnel isn't in the jug.

How can I direct my attention to the problem at hand?

Let's see how a writer of fiction manages to direct your attention to his story. You know what happens when the author fails to direct your attention—you lay the book aside or turn to another story.

How does the fiction writer get you interested in his story?

1. Action

He may start the story with action—plenty of action. Somebody is getting killed or about to get killed. Bullets are flying, knives are slashing, and blood is flowing.

There is one cue for you. Direct your attention to a new problem by plunging into action, either mental action, physical action, or both. Don't play around the edge of the new problem—plunge right in and begin to solve it.

2. Wants

The great masters of fiction can draw your attention to their story with just a few simple descriptive sentences. How? They build a situation wherein you want something to happen. Once you want something to happen, you are into the story. You are no longer reading the story—you are living it vicariously.

It is much the same in life—once you want something you begin living. And when you want something and jump into action to get it, your attention is directed to the means whereby you intend to satisfy that want.

Suppose you want food. If the food is lying in front of you so that all you have to do is to reach out, pick it up, and start eating, the problem is so simple that there is no possible chance for confusing your motives. In such situations your action can hardly fail to be effective.

It is in the more complicated problems that must be broken down into steps and each step performed in proper sequence that you and I very often run into trouble.

To solve such problems effectively we must identify our ultimate goal with the step at hand so that the step at hand attracts our attention just as much as the final goal. We must realize that for the moment the step at hand is more important to us than the final goal, since if we muff this step we may lose all opportunity to achieve our ultimate end. Or we may feel that the step at hand is not nearly so important to us as some step that lies ahead of us. Here again we must realize that unless we perform the step at hand in a satisfactory manner we may never have the opportunity to solve the steps ahead; therefore, the step at hand is for the moment the only thing of any importance to us.

Most flying students cannot understand why their instructor places so much emphasis upon their approach to a landing. To the student flier the landing seems so important that maintaining the proper uniform speed during the glide seems trivial by comparison—on the approach his attention is not on what he is doing but upon the problem of the landing that lies ahead of him. As a result he either undershoots or overshoots the spot on which he wishes to land, or he reaches that point with either too much speed or too little speed and consequently experiences great difficulty in landing.

The situation grows worse instead of improving. The fact that he had difficulty in landing and apparently experienced no difficulty during the approach to the landing convinces the student that he need only worry about the landing, that the approach can take care of itself.

Worrying about the landing in advance does not improve his likelihood of making a good landing.

He fails to make the proper approach because his full attention is not directed to the problem of the approach, and he fails to realize that his instructor means what he says: "You make bad landings because of your sloppy approach. Develop the proper approach and the landings will take care of themselves."

The Four-Engine Combat Crew School, located at the

Army Air Base at Smyrna, Tennessee, developed a technique of approach that practically did away with the necessity for making a landing. If this approach was properly executed, the landing took place as a culmination of the approach.

It was during World War II. There was a shortage of B-24 pilots. There was a shortage of B-24's available for training purposes. There was a shortage of gasoline and a shortage of rubber. It became essential to speed up the training of pilots to land the heavy bombers. This resulted in the adoption o£ a unique method of approach.

The pilot turned on the final approach at a point one thousand feet above the ground and three miles from the end of the runway on which he was to land. He pointed the nose of the airplane directly at the end of the runway and kept it pointed at the end of the runway throughout the approach. Then he maintained the desired air speed by the application of power through use of the throttles. He lowered the flaps in stages until he had full flap. As he approached the runway he decreased the air speed by stages until, when he crossed the end of the runway, the airplane was at just the right angle of attack for a perfect landing, with the speed just a few miles an hour above the landing speed of the airplane. Then, all the pilot had to do was to close the four throttles and ease back just a trifle on the wheel as the giant bomber settled onto the runway—it was easier than landing a cub.

These pilots, however, had to keep their minds on each step in turn as they made their approach, for if they muffed any one step all the steps ahead would also suffer.

The final execution of the landing became the simplest part of the entire procedure—maintaining the proper air speed throughout the approach was the all-important factor.

This same principle applies to any landing. The ability to make a good approach in turn depends upon learning to make uniform glides and turns long before the student even begins to practice landings. Instructors who place the proper emphasis upon the student's air-work save the undercarriage of the airplane from a lot of wear and tear.

## HOW CAN I HOLD MY ATTENTION TO THE PROBLEM AT HAND?

Again we will observe the skillful writer to see how he holds your attention to his story.

1. Continuous Progress Toward the Goal

The writer must keep the story in motion and all action must lead toward the attainment of the final goal. Here is a valuable cue for you. Keep right at your problem. Keep acting either mentally or physically toward the solution of the problem.

Some writers love to indulge in little philosophies of their own aside from the theme or thread of the story; philosophies that do not serve to move the story ahead toward a final solution. Regardless of how interesting such asides may be, the reader finds his attention being drawn from the story. When you indulge in a little thought as to what your instructor thinks of you or try to estimate your rate of progress compared with that of your fellow students, your attention is drawn away from the problem at hand. A little daydreaming will really get you away from your problem.

2. The Will-to-Win

If you reach a point in the story where you do not care whether the hero wins or not, you lose interest in the story. An intense desire to see the hero win rivets your attention to the story. In like manner an intense will-to-win holds your attention to the problem at hand.

In any activity you and I undertake we have two rewards awaiting us if we succeed.

(a) The prize that we are actually working for.

(b) The satisfaction that we derive from success—from accomplishing what we set out to do—from winning.

It is just possible that this will-to-win may be the key to holding your attention to the step at hand.

Suppose you are playing poker for high stakes. If you win, let's say you will be $100 richer.

Now we will grant that you may actually enjoy the $100 a great deal more than you will enjoy the satisfaction of winning. But which is the most effective incentive, the $100 or the desire to win?

If the $100 is your incentive, your mind may be on the $100 as you play instead of on the game. Consequently you play a poor game and are likely to lose unless exceedingly lucky.

If the desire to win is your incentive, your mind will be on the game itself with the result that you play a good game and are more likely to win if you have a decent run of luck.

How can a person develop this will-to-win?

By training ourselves to make this effort to win, we can no doubt go a long way toward developing a will-to-win. However, more important is the experience of actually winning. This is what makes it tough. You have to win before you can realize the full satisfaction that comes to you from winning. Fortunately, most of us can win at something, and the wise flying instructor sees to it that his students do win, even if he has to whittle down the size of the problem by breaking it into easier steps.

3. By Avoiding Undue Fatigue and Maintaining a State of Health So That Your Nervous System Functions Swiftly and Effectively

A writer can't do much about this point, but you know that, if you are tired or suffering from some illness, you may lose interest in the middle of an interesting story and lay the book or magazine aside. These same factors of fatigue and illness detract from our ability to hold our attention to the problem at hand.

We discover a clue as to why fatigue and poor health lessen our ability to concentrate on the problem at hand through a study of the effects of certain drugs that stimulate the central nervous system. These drugs make it easier, for the time being, for an individual to hold his attention to the problem at hand. Why? Because these drugs increase the speed at which nerve impulses go hurtling along the neurons and across the synapses (the junctions between nerve cells) . They relieve fatigue.

Physiologists explain it this way: When a nerve cell is continuously stimulated, it becomes bored, and its refractory period—the period when it will not react to a stimuli lengthens. It also seems that the by-products of metabolism that accumulate in the area of the synapses when a nerve is continuously stimulated interfere with the transmission of the impulse across the synapse to the next nerve cell. Hence, when nerve cells are subjected to continuous stimulation, we find nerve impulses blocked. When such a situation develops, the attention is likely to wander. Perhaps some of the activity may be transferred to pathways that are not bored by such continuous stimulation.

That is why drugs that stimulate the central nervous system also aid the individual in his ability to hold his attention.

Fatigue, lack of sleep, illness, worry, and grave forebodings all contribute to a condition in which nerve impulses travel more slowly and are occasionally blocked at the synapses. Consequently these conditions detract from our ability to hold our attention to the problem at hand.

It is not so much our capacity for effective action as it is our ability to direct our efforts to the problem at hand that leads to success. We seem to be much like the modern motor car, in that there doesn't seem to be such a great difference between makes. Most any make of modern motor car will give reasonably good service if it is driven carefully and properly cared for.

Most any individual can make a success of life if he properly directs his attention and holds to the road. It is equally true that most of us fail to direct our attention and we allow ourselves to leave the highway that leads to success.

I.Q. tests, developed by psychologists, have shown a remarkable similarity in the mental capacity of people. I.Q. stands for intelligence quotient. An I.Q. of 100 represents the intelligence of the average or normal individual, age being taken into consideration.

Suppose we examine the records of thousands upon thousands of such tests that have been recorded, in an effort to determine how intelligence is distributed among the human race on a percentage basis.

IQ Range                    Percentage of the Population Found in Each Range

Below 68........................... 2

68 to 83........................... 14

84 to 116........................... 68

117 to 132..........................14

Above 132   ........................2

Notice how little we vary in actual intellectual capacity. About 2% in the feeble-minded class and about 2% in the genius class. About 14% are a little above average and about 14% are a little below average, while in a narrow range that we might consider average we find 68%.

Since this ability to direct our attention seems to be so important to our success, let's take a look at it from a negative point of view. Yes, there are times when it is desirable to scatter our attention, to allow our thoughts to wander. We do this when we want to sleep.

It is difficult to go to sleep when our attention is directed to some problem or when some loud noise or some other sensory stimulus directs our attention to our environment.

Our thoughts can disturb us by directing our attention to certain problems. We switch our thoughts to matters of less consequence, preferably to something pleasant, and allow these thoughts to wander. When our thoughts begin to wander we know that we will soon be asleep, for, as they wander to more and more things, never stopping on any one detail long enough to accomplish anything, awareness fades and we fall asleep.

If we are tired or fatigued, we become sleepy, since the mental processes are working more slowly and it is less likely that we will hold our attention to anything. In fact, if our mental processes are working slowly enough we find it almost impossible to direct or hold our attention to anything and we fall asleep.

In just such a fatigued situation as we have described, certain drugs that stimulate the central nervous system will keep us awake by making it easier to direct and hold our attention.

Wouldn't it be nice if our body manufactured such a drug and would inject it into our blood whenever we needed to direct and hold our attention to some problem? Strangely enough, the body does manufacture just such a drug and does secrete it into the blood in increasing amounts whenever there is need for action.

Sitting atop the kidneys like cocked hats are two little glands known as the adrenals. The medulla of these glands produces a secretion known as adrenin. The proprietary name for the synthetic drug with the same characteristics is Adrenalin.

Adrenin is a drug that speeds the mental processes. Our emotions cause the adrenals to increase their production of adrenin. One of the most powerful of our emotions is the will-to-win. Athletes have been known to drop dead on the athletic field because an intense will-to-win caused such an overproduction of adrenin that its effects caused death through overexertion.

Every act that you and I put forth is a response evoked by stimuli acting through one of our physiological drives. Stimuli from our external environment are integrated with stimuli from our internal environment, and the pattern of stimuli resulting from this integration follows a neural pathway known as a physiological drive to a point where some response is evoked.

These physiological drives are fixed neural pathways through which a response is evoked for the purpose of fulfilling our physiological needs. Through a process of learning that we call conditioning we build motivations upon these fixed pathways. If we think of the physiological drive as a river flowing to response, we can think of the motivation as a tributary that flows into the physiological drive.

Motivations are specialized means of fulfilling our

physiological needs. For instance, food is one of our physiological needs, and hunger is a physiological drive to seek food.

You and I have discovered that we have more success in our efforts to secure food if we have a pocketful of money. Hence money becomes a specialized means of seeking food, and the motivation to earn money is a motivation built upon the physiological drive to seek food.

A scientist may discover that if he develops a process that will reduce substantially the cost of producing a certain article he will be in possession of knowledge that he can exchange for money. Thus the desire to acquire this precious bit of knowledge may also be a motivation built upon the motivation to earn money.

Somewhere along the way, however, this scientist has learned to enjoy the satisfaction of solving a problem so that the will-to-win may have become the strongest of his motivations. The desire to earn money might not be powerful enough to drive him to all the effort necessary to the solving of this problem, but there is no limit to the effort that the will-to-win may produce.

The will-to-win does more to make action effective than any other motivation because it directs our attention to the act itself, for the goal of the will-to-win is to perform the act successfully.

Our other motivations are built up in such a complex manner that they often lead us to confusing, false goals. It is even more likely that our motivations may direct our attention to the ultimate end rather than to the act we are performing, through directing our attention to the prizes that we gain by succeeding rather than to the satisfaction that we obtain from the act of winning.

Let's see how one may get mixed up so that he fails to direct his attention to the step at hand:

Johnny wants to become a good basketball player. This motivation is built upon other motivations; the desire to have people respect and think well of him and, possibly, the desire to win the love and affection of Suzie Perkins. Becoming a capable basketball player is the means that Johnny intends to use to fulfill these other motivations.

There is nothing wrong in seeking the prizes and there is nothing wrong with the means used by Johnny in seeking the prizes.

If Johnny becomes a good basketball player he will automatically gain the respect of his fellows and perhaps win Suzie as well. Thus he can temporarily forget these prizes of success and concentrate upon playing good basketball. It is important that he keep his attention upon the means by which he will attain his ends rather than upon the ends themselves.

The big game is on. Johnny is in the clear with a clean shot at the basket open to him. But he is thinking, "This will make them admire me; this will impress Suzie." He looks to see if Suzie is watching him and, in that instant, one of his opponents moves in and his shot at the basket is blocked. He lost out because he did not keep his attention on the means to the end but allowed it to dwell upon the end itself. He took the funnel out of the jug.

Let's look at it another way. Johnny wants his team to win. Again his motive is to win Suzie and the respect and admiration of his fellows. If the team wins, he, as a member of the team, will win that respect and admiration. All he has to do is to keep his attention on winning the game, to make every effort count in that direction.

But what does he do? He forgets that the big thing is to win the game. He wants to impress Suzie, and now seems a good time to do it. So he starts grandstanding; he shoots from the middle of the floor and misses when he should have passed the ball to one of his team-mates. The game is lost, and everyone says it is due to Johnny's showing off. He has lost the very admiration and respect which he coveted, and perhaps Suzie as well. Had he kept his attention on the more specialized motivation, the means to the end, the winning of the game, he could have attained all those things he desired. As it was, by allowing the prizes to steal his attention, he lost them.

It is much the same when one is learning to fly. It is natural for anyone to want his instructor to think he is a hot-shot. It is a good thing for anyone to want to be the best. It is desirable for anyone to want to learn quickly. It is well for anyone to desire the respect and admiration of his fellows.

He can win these prizes of success if he does a good job of flying, but if he directs his attention to the prizes themselves he is directing his efforts into futile, wasteful channels and is likely to fail. When he directs his full attention to learning to fly and to the particular step that is at hand, he is keeping the funnel in the jug. He is directing his efforts into the channels through which they will bring success.

The entire problem of directing our attention to the act that we are performing is complicated by the necessity to divert a portion of our attention from this act to a step that we are performing simultaneously, the planning of our action. Planning is one of the essential steps, and the mind skips back and forth between the performance of the act and planning ahead for future action.

1. By breaking down problems to a step-by-step procedure in advance, we find less necessity for planning on the spot, leaving more of our attention available for performing the act.

2. Through training we can develop automatic reflexes, similar to walking, that require little conscious attention.

3. Through study—training our minds to solve the particular problems that are continually involved in flying—we can develop automatic mental reflexes similar to our physical reflexes. These mental reflexes will enable our minds to make a wide range of associations with but little conscious effort upon our part.

Many of us unconsciously assume that we are such brilliant supermen that we can save a lot of needless effort by waiting until we are in the situation, and then doing all of our planning as we act. By neglecting to prepare in advance we place such a peak load upon our mental capacities in the critical moments of life that we are not likely to act effectively.

We can compare ourselves to a power company that can get a greater output from its equipment through distributing its output to avoid high peak loads. With us, as with the power company, we find that these high peak loads are likely to cause the equipment to break down.

Through preparation we distribute the load on our mental capacity so that we avoid overloads in the critical moments of life.

Suppose we analyze a complicated bit of activity: We will suppose that a pilot takes off from St. Louis headed for Chicago without planning his flight and without studying the weather. His motor begins malfunctioning en route and at the same time he encounters a severe storm. He has several problems:

1.  The normal operation of the airplane can be largely taken care of by his automatic reflexes, with little attention upon his part, if he has been well trained.

2.  As for the problem of dealing with the malfunctioning motor, if he has studied motors and understands them, his automatic mental reflexes will aid him so that he will not require much conscious attention in dealing with this problem.

3.  As for deciding what to do about the storm, here again if he has studied meteorology so that he understands something of the nature of storms, his automatic mental reflexes can relieve some of the load on his conscious attention.

4.  In case he cannot get through the storm, he has the problem of planning his return flight to St. Louis, an alternate course to Peoria, Illinois, or an alternate course to Kankakee, Illinois. As in the two preceding problems, if he is well experienced in navigation and can lay out a flight plan with ease, his automatic mental reflexes can relieve him of much conscious attention.

If his mind cannot meet all of these problems, he may adopt a pattern of action directed by his emotions. In such a case we commonly say, "He got caught with his pants down." He will be fortunate in such circumstances if he does not meet with disaster.

The inexperienced pilot who is not so well endowed with a host of automatic mental reflexes need not "Stick his neck out" or "Get caught out on the end of a limb."

Before leaving St. Louis he can study the weather with care and plan a number of alternate procedures that he can select from and adapt to the situation he encounters.

Before he takes off from St. Louis he can make a careful, detailed flight plan that includes the return flight to St. Louis if he finds that an 180-degree turn is advisable. He can also prepare alternate flight plans to Peoria, Illinois, and Kankakee, Illinois, if it seems wise to alter his course to either of these two cities. With his flight planned in this manner, his attention will not be so severely divided when he encounters difficulties.

Through painstaking preparation, the experienced pilot can establish a reputation for reliable performance that will place him at the top of his profession.

Worrying about a future step, once we have it planned, is not necessary and wastes our efforts through a needless division of our attention.

We have been studying the factors that are involved in absent-mindedness. Absent-mindedness merely means that our mind is absent from the problem at hand. Absent-mindedness is a deadly foe to effective action, but we ordinarily think of absent-mindedness as a condition wherein the person has his attention centered on some previous problem, having failed to shift his attention to the problem that confronts him at the moment. This was the case with Jake when he failed to notice that the control stick was missing.

However, we are also absent-minded when worrying about the ultimate end or some step that lies ahead, or when our attention is on some irrelevant phase of the problem or upon some false goal. Such absent-mindedness is just as likely to cause us to fumble and stumble as is the variety of absent-mindedness that is so unjustly associated with college professors.

Insufficient planning can lead us into situations where we must divide our attention among too many problems, so that we put on a poor performance.

# 5

# Learning to Relax

"You've gotta relax! Dammit!" Such words, which so often explode from the lips of flying instructors, are not helpful to tense, high-strung students.

Well, why should you relax? The muscles of the skeletal system are paired, so that the contraction of one of the muscles will move the member in one direction and the contraction of the opposing muscle will move the member in the opposite direction. Normally, when one muscle contracts, the opposing muscle relaxes. But, if you wish to hold that member stiff and rigid, you contract both muscles.

When we contract these two opposing muscles we say that we tense them, that is, there is a tension between them. Our muscles possess a certain amount of this tenseness, which is often spoken of as muscle tone. It serves to hold us in shape, as opposing guy wires hold a flagpole erect. Were it not for muscle tone, we would collapse like a pup tent whose poles have been struck.

This tenseness, or muscle tone, also seems to favor quick muscular response. Our sympathetic emotions which prepare us for action by marshaling the resources of the body also increase this tenseness, still further preparing us for quick, adaptive action.

You have observed how tense a cat becomes when it is about to spring upon the unhappy mouse. Then why isn't it desirable for us to tense as the cat does, when we wish to be alert, as in flying?

Here is the reason: We have a great many reflex actions which ordinarily are inhibited by the cerebral cortex. Many of them are highly undesirable if they occur when we are flying, since they interfere with our conditioned reflexes, which are acts that we have learned in order to fly.

When you become tense, the cerebral cortex is diverting stimuli to maintain this tenseness, thereby losing some of its inhibiting power over reflex acts which would interfere with our flying. This loss of control is bad because it is highly desirable that we inhibit these undesirable actions. Otherwise, we become jumpy.

You can easily prove this to yourself. You are familiar with the knee-jerk, known as the patellar reflex. Cross your legs and tap the knee, just below the knee-cap, and notice the amount of knee-jerk produced. Now tense your fists and forearms as tightly as possible. Have someone tap just below your knee-cap, and notice the amount of knee-jerk you get this time. You will find that your foot will kick up more violently and much higher this time. The cerebral cortex diverted so much stimuli to tense the muscles in your forearms and fists that it had less ability to inhibit this simple reflex act.

Furthermore, your emotions flow more smoothly when you are physically relaxed. Hence you will learn faster and enjoy smoother flying, if you learn to relax.

Tenseness has a tendency to spread. You can prove this by relaxing your left hand and then clenching your right fist as tightly as possible. Notice how the relaxed fingers of the left hand tend to start curling slightly, as though trying to clench into a fist too. When you relax any tense part of your body, you will find that there is a tendency toward general relaxation at the same time, and, conversely, when you tense any member, you will find a general tendency toward tenseness throughout the body.

If you are flying with your right hand on the controls, allow the other hand to lie limply in your lap. Never clutch some structural member, such as a longeron. When I discovered that a student was clutching the controls with a death grip, I would give him a thin-shelled egg to hold in his free hand throughout the lesson. After breaking a few eggs a student invariably learned to relax his grip on the controls. He simply couldn't grip the control stick so tightly, without also tightening his grip on the egg to the point where he would break it, and, in trying to hold the egg lightly, he also learned to maintain a light, firm hold on the control stick.

Without realizing it, many students, and some experienced pilots, exert a tremendous pressure on the rudder controls with their feet, pushing forward with many pounds of pressure, with both feet at the same time. It's a good thing the rudder controls are securely mounted, or such individuals would shear them off.

I have known students to complain of stiffness in their legs the day after a long flight. No wonder, when they were continually exerting such tremendous pressure against the rudder controls. Placing the heels on the floor boards and the balls of the feet on the rudder controls tends to discourage such tenseness.

At the time I was using the egg trick, I had a mechanic working for me who delighted in inventing and rigging up gadgets. He came up with a neat little device to break a student's habit of applying this great pressure on the rudder controls.

His gadget consisted of switches with their contacts held apart by a spring. One of these switches was mounted on each rudder pedal so that the student's foot operated the switch in applying pressure to the rudder. The two switches were so wired that a circuit would not be completed unless the contacts of both switches were pushed together at the same time. No circuit was formed by the normal operation of the rudder controls, but, when the student tensed and pushed ahead with both feet at the same time, a circuit was formed, and current from a small coil gave the student a rude shock from a metal plate mounted on the seat cushion. We had a lot of fun with this gadget, and it proved successful in teaching the student to relax.

A pilot's posture in the seat may also be too tense. You don't need to slump down like a sack of beans, but neither should you assume the attitude of a marble statue in splints. One should also avoid allowing the muscles of his neck to become too tense. Some people suffer from headaches at the back and top of the head, simply from holding the neck muscles too tense.

As the result of blasphemous cajoling on the part of the drill sergeant in the Army, most new recruits tensed up in terrific fashion when attempting to stand at attention. Many times I have seen men pass out and fall to the ground when standing at attention, which clearly demonstrates the fatiguing effects of tenseness. The pilot who is tense will tire himself much more quickly and may become dangerously fatigued on long flights.

To sum up: The pilot should practice tensing and relaxing various muscles in turn so that he may be able to recognize tenseness. Then when flying he should watch for signs of tenseness, particularly in the muscles of the arms and legs. When such tenseness is observed, he should make an effort to relax. The student should have the instructor demonstrate the difference between a firm, easy hold on the controls, and grasping them with the grip of a drowning man.

Muscular relaxation makes emotional relaxation easier, and emotional relaxation makes muscular relaxation easier.

To understand what we mean by emotional relaxation we will observe two individuals in the same circumstances, one emotionally relaxed and the other emotionally tense.

Your house is on fire. You dash madly from room to room. There are a thousand things you want to do—you start to do one thing and then change your mind and start to do something different. You wonder if your fire insurance is paid up. Where will you live now? How much will it cost to build a new house? What will your wife say, when she comes home and finds a heap of smoldering ashes where the house stood? How in the world did it catch fire?

You bolt upstairs and fling your typewriter, a grandfather clock, and a delicate Ming vase out the window; then you carry a feather mattress carefully downstairs and out onto the lawn.

You try to be everywhere at once, to do everything at once, and succeed in doing very little. You interfere with the firemen and hinder your friends who are trying to help you, saying, "No! Not that! Take the davenport first. Hell! Drop the davenport—let's get the ice box out right now."

Now let's see how you will behave under the same circumstances if you are emotionally relaxed.

You deliberately force yourself to keep your mind on the problems at hand and to work systematically. You don't interfere with the firemen for you know they understand their job better than you do. Your movements may be swift, but you will avoid racing aimlessly about. You will carry fragile articles out and heave the more indestructible things out the window.

In the latter case your emotions flowed smoothly. In the former case they burst out in a conflicting, turbulent mass.

One form of relaxation must be avoided—mental relaxation. When flying you must be mentally alert, with your attention directed to the problem at hand.

Mental alertness favors emotional relaxation. You can easily convince yourself of this if you don't value your life too highly. Try crossing a busy city street when mentally relaxed, thinking about nothing in particular, save perhaps an idle daydream, and see how high you jump, and how madly your heart hammers when an automobile horn suddenly blares at your immediate rear.

Now cross the same street mentally alert and notice how slight an emotional reaction the blaring of an automobile horn produces.

The flying student can aid emotional relaxation by keeping his attention directed to the problem at hand. Here is how he can flood himself with emotions and become emotionally tense:

He can be questioning the methods of his flying instructor: "Is he holding me back?" or "Gosh! I ought to be on landings by now—Jim is, and we both started at the same time."

He is still more likely to be wondering what his instructor

thinks about his progress. "Oh, Lord! He must think I'm dumb. I'll bet I'm the most stupid student he ever taught."

Then he begins thinking up alibis: "You see, my legs are a little short. I think I need a cushion behind me." "You sure surprised me when you asked for a right turn—that's how I came to muff it so badly. Really, I can make a good turn, but the sun was in my eyes." "Don't you think this crate is a little wing-heavy?"

Then he begins comparing himself with other students: "They all seem to be learning faster than I am. Guess I'm the dumbbell of the outfit. I hope they don't notice it. Why does Harry master this thing so well while I do so poorly? I'm smarter than he is."

Or he may be recriminating himself: "Dammit! Why did I do that? Gosh! That was sure a lousy turn."

Or he may be estimating his rate of progress: "It's taking me a long time to catch on to these climbing turns. I wonder if I'm hopeless? It's going to take me thirty hours to solo at this rate."

His mind darts every place but where it should be. He is dividing his attention to such an extent that he is slowing his own progress as well as building emotional tenseness. He's doing everything he possibly can to defeat himself—except, possibly, wanging his instructor over the head with a fire extinguisher; and it wouldn't surprise the instructor if he did that too.

We have just described one of the neatest methods known for defeating one's self in any activity in life. It's infallible and can always be counted on to make you fail in that endeavor in which you want most to succeed.

It is unfortunate that we are not equipped with a switch that we could snap to shut off such a destructive flow of thoughts. But this we can do: We can convince ourselves that learning to fly is the only thing that is important. We can convince ourselves that these other things aren't important; that they don't matter.

No flying instructor will deliberately retard the progress of a student. It doesn't make any difference what the instructor does think of him. The instructor knows that all people don't learn with the same rapidity. He expects a student to make mistakes. If the student's legs are too short, he can put a cushion behind his back on the next flight. There will be other times when the sun will be in his eyes. All that it is important for the student to do is to take one step at a time, and he will progress. It makes no difference how his progress compares with that of other students. Suppose there were no other students?

We may be sure of one thing; our motivations direct our attention in all that we do. The strongest motivation will win out as surely as day follows night. All we can do is to analyze our motivations and put them into their correct place. If it means more to solo next Tuesday than to become a good pilot, our attention will be directed toward soloing next Tuesday rather than to becoming a good pilot.

The instructor can aid the student in relaxing. He can talk in a smooth, even tone of voice rather than shout out orders in staccato fashion. He can praise the best points of a student's flying, by dwelling enthusiastically on the things he does well, while tactfully pointing out his mistakes. "You sure held to the pylons in those eights, though you are still allowing the nose to rise a little on those right turns. But we'll work on that tomorrow till we get it smoothed out." This kind of instruction aids the tense student in relaxing.

The instructor who enjoys pouring out scathing, sarcastic criticism and ridiculing the student before the other students is often deservingly repaid by a student who cannot relax and becomes something of a problem.

Above all, the instructor should try to make the student realize that they are friends. One can always relax more easily among friends, since one doesn't worry so much about what a true friend thinks about him, for he knows that a friend is one who knows his shortcomings and likes him just the same.

That should be the position of the instructor—a friend. Of

course he knows the student's shortcomings and notices his mistakes—that's his job. He wouldn't be a very capable instructor if he didn't. But such knowledge doesn't affect his regard or friendship for the student in the slightest degree.

It isn't all up to the instructor. The student makes a lot of his own mental attitude. If he is suspicious of his instructor and doesn't trust him, he will quite likely believe that his instructor is suspicious of him. If he dislikes his instructor, he will quite naturally think that his instructor dislikes him in turn. If he has a warm, friendly feeling for his instructor, it is quite natural that he should believe that his instructor feels the same way toward him.

Maybe it's because we're so used to looking in mirrors that we feel that others reciprocate our feelings. Perhaps it is from our experience in life. We find that when we smile at a man he generally smiles back, just the same as the mirror does.

When one directs his attention to the problem at hand he shuts out many disturbing stimuli and eliminates most of the emotions that would disturb him and interfere with his efficiency.

We are reminded of the story of the bashful boy from the country, who took his girl friend to the city for an outing. His heart was full of the yearning of young love, but he couldn't find any place to be alone with her. They parked on a busy street, and he was too bashful to slip his arm around her or to sneak a quick kiss with so many people watching.

Finally he hit upon an idea. "Let's crawl under the car with some wrenches and a hammer. I can tap on the muffler occasionally and no one will suspect but what we are repairing the car."

It seemed to be working out pretty well until a policeman began prodding the boy with his night stick.

"Go away and leave us alone. Can't you see we are busy fixing the car?" pleaded the boy.

"I know," replied the policeman, "but what you don't know is that it's pouring down rain, a crowd of 1000 people is holding up traffic to watch you, and someone has stolen your car."

If you and I could direct our attention to the problem at hand as effectively as this couple were doing, we would be unaware of many of the unpleasant, nagging distractions that bring us so much unhappiness and ruin our effectiveness.

To sum up: When a man is tense he is set for something to happen, like a cat waiting for a mouse to appear. Such an attitude serves a useful purpose when directed toward a real and worth-while problem at a time when we are devoting our efforts to solving such a problem.

When we get set for things to happen which really don't matter, which are molehills built into mountains by our imagination, we become so tense that we become jumpy—a simple way of saying that our primitive reflexes take over, detracting from the efficiency of intelligent action.

Such a condition of tenseness tends to spread and to grow. Fortunately we can diminish it in the same progressive manner by attacking it at any point where we observe it. Usually we are more aware of its physical manifestations, in the tensing of opposing muscles which tend to make the body rigid. In relaxing any rigid member of the body we find that this relaxation also tends to spread.

Since emotional tenseness is very often due to a mass of conflicting emotions, we can reduce this tenseness by directing our attention to the one real motivation of the moment, the problem at hand, and forgetting the distracting side motivations. When the problem at hand is a step in solving a problem; when it is but a means to an end; then we will do well to keep our attention from straying to the end, since doing this may cause us to fail in the step essential to reaching that end.

For example: You are crossing a stream, stepping from stone to stone. You need not look at the opposite bank, for so long as you step on each stone in turn you know that you will eventually get there. Your girl friend on the opposite shore shouts, "Hurry up!" You switch your gaze from the stone on which you are about to step, to the opposite shore, and in that moment your foot misses the stone and you plunge into the swirling waters.

Mental alertness favors emotional and physical relaxation.

Such tenseness as may result from mental alertness is directed to the problem at hand and aids in solving the problem.

When you get set for something that may be logically expected to happen in the solving of the problem at hand, the energies of your body are being marshaled for an intelligent response.

When you get set for a dozen things that bear no relation to the problem at hand and will most likely never occur, you not only diminish your effectiveness for intelligent action, but encourage many worthless reflex responses, which may actually block and interfere with intelligent action.

We cannot relax by turning off a switch. We cannot say, "I must relax," and find ourselves relaxed as a result of a mental command.

We relax as we would put out a forest fire; by stamping out the flames wherever we find them, by relaxing tense muscles, wherever and whenever we observe them. Often we get the very best results by setting a backfire, through directing and holding our attention to the problem at hand.

# 6
# Learning to Observe

The roar of a powerful motor, pulsing out of the murky night of early winter, came from an airliner en route from Kansas City to Chicago. As the airliner passed over the broad Mississippi, the pilot noticed that ice was beginning to form on the wings. The ice formation grew at an alarming rate.

The dim pattern of lights outlining the airport of Kewanee, Illinois, was a welcome sight to the anxious pilot. It was a small irregular field, not a regular stop, and much too small for the huge plane he was flying, but he skillfully set the plane down just a few feet within the boundary limits of the field.

He applied the brakes and was horrified to discover that they were not effective on the sod surface wrapped in a glaze of frost. The plane slid along for several hundred feet.

The pilot's heart sank as the landing lights revealed the fence at the far boundary of the field. He realized that he would be unable to stop the airliner soon enough to avoid crashing through the fence.

He decided to pour on the coal and take off again. He didn't quite clear the fence, and the propeller sliced one of the steel fence posts as though it were made of cheese. The plane hurtled across the highway, still under full power. A portion of the tail surfaces was left hanging on one of the solid fence posts, from which hung a gate to a driveway leading to a farmyard.

The plane passed between the house and a windmill with only inches to spare, then crashed into a crib filled with corn.

Four passengers were killed. The pilot was bruised and scratched, but miraculously escaped serious injury. His worst ordeal lay ahead of him.

When questioned as to why he had undertaken the unsuccessful attempt to take off, he replied, "There were green lights ahead of me and I did not expect to encounter any obstructions."

His questioners were startled by this revelation. They looked significantly at each other, then turned to stare in their disbelief at the pilot. There had been no colored lights of any kind marking the boundaries of the airport that night; just the plain, white boundary lights.

The pilot insisted that there had been green lights ahead of him.

One of his questioners remarked, "Hell, there isn't a green light on the field, with the exception of the green marker on the beacon tower, to show that the beacon is located on or near an airport."

This chance remark solved the riddle. We all knew that the pilot was not deliberately lying. With his mind on the problem of setting the huge plane down in the limited space, the pilot had not looked too carefully. His eyes caught a bit of green—the light on the beacon tower on the corner of the airport ahead—and his mind filled in the green lights which he wanted to see and fully expected to see.

Our visual perception is improved through the fact that the mind often fills in gaps with bits from our past experience to complete the picture, and we see more than is actually reflected on the retina of the eye.

Sometimes the actual stimuli brought to the brain from the retina of the eye are incomplete and do not contain all the elements of the picture which we expect to see. But if there are enough clues to correspond to what our background of experience tells us we should see, then our mind fills in the gaps and we see a complete picture.

Remember those stencils the teacher placed against the blackboard and dusted with an eraser when you were in the first grade? Then you drew in the lines between the dots to complete the picture. That is what our mind so often does with the incomplete stimuli brought to it from the eye.

One of the best examples of this phenomenon is furnished

74

by the adult who almost needs glasses. He can read a magazine with ease. The print seems clear. But when he comes to the bottom of the page, and a notation says "turn to page 97," he is lost. The number, even though it is the same size as the print, seems a hazy blur and he cannot make it out. The same thing is true of the numbers at the top of the page. He may have to make several attempts before he finally succeeds in turning to the proper page.

In reading, the print is reflected as an indistinct blurred image on the retina of the eye, but the mind has a great background of experience in reading; it is accustomed to the various sequences of letters, the sequences of vowels and consonants, the sequences of words themselves: all the common combinations of letters, so that the mind can quickly fill in the gaps and the print appears clear to the reader.

There is not much about a number to provide such a clue. There is no reason why 9 and 7 should go together on this particular occasion; consequently, the mind finds it difficult to fill in the gaps.

One of the students of modern psychology had been nearly blind all his life. Someone had to read to him. But he so skillfully trained his mind to fill in the gaps that today, when his vision should normally be growing less acute, he is able to read without the aid of glasses.

Suppose we compare a student and an Indian guide who has never learned to read, but who, so far as the eye is concerned, possesses the same acuity of vision. Print on the page of a magazine might appear clear to the student but indistinct and blurred to the Indian. Yet this same Indian could look at tracks which the student couldn't see at all, because here the Indian possesses a background of experience capable of filling in the gaps. There may be only indistinct traces, but he sees clear-cut tracks.

This ability of the mind to fill in increases the range of our perception but it may also deceive us at times. That is why, when much depends on what we see, we must learn to take a second, careful look.

You snap the shutter of a camera, and all that is within the range of the lens appears in the picture. But we do not see all that is reflected on the retina of the eye. We see that part to which our attention is directed, and we may be only vaguely aware of the remainder.

Suppose you are sitting in Duffy's Tavern, a pretty blonde at your side, a foamy mug of beer in your hand. Covering the wall before you is an enormous panoramic mural of Ouster's Last Stand. The picture is all within the range of your vision, but you only vaguely see it as a whole. You see an Indian who, with an upraised tomahawk, is about to scalp a soldier. Or perhaps you are looking at a blazing overturned wagon or at an Indian pitching from his horse. Your attention switches from one feature of the picture to another, until finally you are aware of the entire scene.

Our eyes bring us a mass of sensory stimuli in a manner similar to that in which a person may view the panorama of Ouster's Last Stand. As in the case of the picture, we see the whole scene vaguely, and, as we switch our attention from detail to detail, picking out the things which interest us, we finally become aware of the whole scene.

Certain features tend to force themselves upon us. The most striking features are those that indicate motion or change of some kind. Large objects catch our eye. Small objects that are repeated may attract our attention almost as much as the large objects, provided the repetition does not become monotonous.

Striking qualities, such as bright colors, also catch the eye. Our organic state also influences our attention. If we are thirsty, a bubbling spring of water may fascinate us or, if we are hungry, our attention may stray to the soldier's broken knapsack, from which various articles of food are spilling.

Each of us has certain interests that influence our attention. If you are a veterinary or a horse lover, you will probably focus your attention on the horses in the picture. If you are a gunsmith, your attention may be drawn to the guns that the soldiers are firing.

Various social pressures and motivations, which are difficult to trace, also have a great influence upon the direction of our attention. We voluntarily direct our attention when we specialize our interests.

Our various sensory receptors react to various types of change, and they react only to change.

You have suffered from a toothache all night. In the morning you hurry to the dentist to have the offending tooth removed. The dentist asks, "Which tooth is it?"

You don't want the wrong tooth pulled, so you concentrate your attention on the aching tooth and hold it there for some time, just to be sure you make no mistake.

Then a foolish grin spreads across your face. "Hell! Doc! It has stopped aching."

When you held your attention right on that aching tooth, there was not enough change to produce a continuous sensation—it faded, and the ache seemed to have disappeared.

Pain is a poor example of this phenomenon, since pain is changeable because of the heartbeat which produces a constantly changing wave-like flow of blood that causes the pain to throb with the pulse.

The urge to evacuate the bowels is a better example. You are attending a reception, a wedding, or possibly a funeral, when you feel this urge. You put it off and, when the gathering breaks up, you discover that you no longer feel the urge. So long as the urge was becoming greater you could feel it, since there was a change. But when it reached its peak, the feeling disappeared because the sensory receptors are not stimulated by a static condition—only by change.

This is best illustrated by the classic example of the pails of hot, cold, and tepid water. You dip your hand in the tepid water and can scarcely feel it; you feel only the sensation of the contact with the water because there is no change between the temperature of the surrounding air and the water.

You dip your hand in the hot water and wince with the pain, but in a couple of minutes the water no longer feels hot, although there has been no change in its temperature.

You dip your other hand in the cold water and you may gasp from the cold. But leave it there a few minutes, and you will not feel the cold any longer, although the water is just as cold as when you first dipped your hand in it.

Now take the one hand out of the hot water and the other out of the cold water, and plunge them both into the pail of tepid water. To the hand that you removed from the hot water, the tepid water feels cold, and to the hand that you removed from the cold water, the tepid water feels hot. Sensory receptors in each hand are faithfully recording a change.

All of our sensory receptors possess this trait of reacting to change and to nothing but change. If you have attended a baseball game at the White Sox Ball Park in Chicago when the wind was blowing from the direction of the stockyards, you may have been sickened by the overpowering stench. However, if it was a steady wind, you soon found the awareness of the stench fading, and later you may have not noticed it at all. But, if the wind was gusty and continually switching from one direction to the other, so that the stench came in waves, you probably were annoyed throughout the game by the sickening stench.

This brings us to a useful device in observing. If we switch our sensory attention, we provide this change and thus increase our powers of perception and our awareness.

When a student is under the hood learning to fly by instruments, he often hears the command from his instructor, "Needle—ball—air speed! Watch the needle! Watch the ball! Watch the air speed!"

The instructor insists that the student shall not allow his attention to center on one instrument.

It is, of course, obvious that if, through keeping the attention overly long on one instrument, the student allows other instruments to get away, he will soon get far behind and wind up madly chasing the instruments all over the panel.

However, there is also another serious possibility. If the student glues his attention to one instrument, his awareness may begin to fade, particularly if there is but little fluctuation of that instrument. Staring ahead in a hypnotic-like trance, he may fail to notice gradual movement of the indicator.

To learn to be observing is to learn to switch your sensory attention continually from one detail to another of the scene before you.

For instance, you are going to draw a straight line from A to B. You will look at the pencil-point which lies on A, and then glance to point B, and to imaginary points in between. Try gluing your attention to one point and see what kind of luck you have drawing a straight line.

Sometimes you move your entire head when switching your visual attention; sometimes just the eyeballs are moved. And again you may change the focus slightly, or the change of attention may be entirely mental.

When you wish to detach yourself from all visual sensory stimuli in order to concentrate on some problem, you need not necessarily close the eyes; you may stare continuously at some object, like a pretty girl on a calendar. Soon the girl will fade from your vision. You are still looking at her, but there is insufficient change to produce awareness. Switch your gaze away, then right back again, and you will again see the girl.

The observant person continually switches his sensory attention from detail to detail of his problem. The unobservant person keeps his attention overly long on each detail.

The military air services and the commercial airlines both have check-lists of things to be checked before starting the motors; a list to be checked while the motors are being warmed up; a pre-take-off check-list; and a list to be checked after power has been reduced and the airplane leveled off for cruising. Then there is a list to be checked before coming in to land, and a list to be checked before leaving the airplane on the flight line.

These check-lists develop the pilot's powers of observation. Through their use, he is forced to look at each detail on the list until fully aware of it and then to switch his attention to the next detail. Eventually it will become a habit, and he might throw aside the check-list, were it not for regulations.

A man learning to become a detective becomes observant in the same manner. He has a list of things to check in certain situations and he checks each quickly and proceeds to the next, thus switching his attention. This switching of attention is the only way you can learn to see details. You miss them entirely when you just stare at the scene before you.

The scientist, by the same sort of check-list, learns to be observant when he peers through his microscope. He checks certain details and then switches his attention to the next detail. Of course, such check-lists need not necessarily be written on a piece of paper; we may carry them in our memory. But where observation must be trained we use such lists, for this method is extremely effective in developing reliable powers of observation. Without such a list we are less likely to switch our attention.

The student pilot could make a list such as this:

(1) Check the longitudinal attitude of the airplane by noting the position of the nose relative to the horizon.

(2) Check the lateral attitude by checking the lines of the nose for parallelism with the horizon. At the start you may have to glance from one wing-tip to the other, noting their relation to the horizon, and then back to the nose.

(3) Check for any turning, the directional attitude of the airplane, by comparing the nose with some check point on the horizon or on the ground ahead for reference.

(4) Check the amount of back or forward pressures you are applying to the controls, just after checking the longitudinal attitude.

(5) Check the side pressure you are applying, just after checking the lateral attitude.

(6)  Check the pressure you are applying to the rudder, just after checking the directional attitude.

(7)  Check for tenseness in the hands and arms.

(8)  Check for tenseness in the legs and feet.

(9)  Check for tenseness in posture.

(10)  Check for airplanes in the vicinity.

Later the student can add to this check-list. He can add the occasional checking of the engine and flight instruments. He can also add a checking of points on the terrain below with corresponding points on his map.

At first this switching of the attention is admittedly difficult to master. The student is so intent on his longitudinal attitude that he doesn't want to take his attention from the relationship between the nose and the horizon for a single moment.

As a result, he loses much of his awareness and may fail to notice that the nose is slowly creeping up above the horizon, until his instructor says, "Watch that nose or you'll soon be in a stall."

If he switches his attention to check other details, he will be more likely to notice any slight change in the position of the nose when his attention swings back to it. He will become aware of any change in the position of the nose more readily than he would if he stared at it. The term staring ahead with unseeing eyes is quite appropriate.

It's like taking snapshots. It is difficult to show distinct motion in one long exposure without getting a blur. But we can take a bunch of snapshots and run them through the motion picture projector and see clear, distinct motion.

Just wanting to be observant, and trying to appear bright-eyed and interested, will not make one observant any more than wanting confidence will give one confidence. Switching the attention over a check-list of important details cannot fail to make one observant, and in time it will become an involuntary habit. In switching our attention over the details of a check-list, we, of course, return more frequently to the important details than to the minor ones.

We are intelligent observers when we know what we are looking for.

You are running up the motor in your airplane. You are listening intently to the loud roar. To you, it sounds OK. Then a skilled mechanic walks over and taps you on the shoulder. You throttle back the motor so that you can hear him. "Sounds like you have an intake leak," he says. Or it may be a connecting-rod knock, a loose tappet, a bad main-bearing thump, or something else which he has detected.

Now, how could he detect this when you couldn't? You were listening too—and the flight surgeon says you have good hearing. But now as you listen . . . sure enough, you hear it too. Suggestion? Not entirely. You heard the sound when you knew what to listen for and switched your attention to it. The mechanic, as he listened, was continually switching his attention, first listening for one sort of sound and then for another, whereas, for all of your straining, all you heard was a loud roar.

The question is frequently asked, "How long should one hold his attention to one detail before switching it to the next?"

The answer is, "Just long enough to be fully aware of what you see, hear, or sense. Once full awareness is reached, it begins to fade."

We have mentioned how this switching the attention from detail to detail can become an involuntary habit which makes one observing. It is important that we point out some limitations to such involuntary checking.

Mrs. Bailey was sitting placidly in church listening to the preacher's sermon when the preacher began to consign some luckless individual to the eternal fires of Hell. Mrs. Bailey immediately thought of the roast in the oven. Did she or did she not turn off the gas under the roast before departing for church?

For the life of her, she could not remember. The more she thought about it, the more likely it seemed that a cloud of black smoke from a badly burned roast must be rising from the oven at that very moment.

Hastily she rose from her seat and, with the curious eyes of the congregation focused upon her, fled from the church and hastened home to take care of the roast. She discovered to her relief that she had turned off the gas.

Before leaving for church she had made her customary routine check to make sure that lights were turned off, that water was not pouring from an open faucet, that the gas was turned off under the roast, and that the front door was locked. This checking was a sort of routine reflex activity on her part, and we do not remember our reflex actions so well. Had she consciously focused her attention on each detail as she performed it, she would probably have remembered making the check.

There is also more likelihood of error entering into our involuntary observations than into those of which we are taking conscious note.

During World War II, I was sent to pick up a twin-engined attack bomber on an airport in the Mojave Desert. The bomber's load was exceedingly heavy, and I was required to make three landings and take-offs to familiarize myself with the heavier load before departing on the cross-country flight.

The temperature was well above a hundred degrees, and full flap was needed to land. I made two landings and take-offs without incident and was making my approach for the final landing. At the edge of the airport, I discovered that I was having difficulty slowing the airplane for the landing. My eyes strayed to the flap indicator, and I saw that my flaps were retracted.

On this particular bomber, the flap actuating lever is to the left, and slightly to the rear of the pilot. He pulls the lever up to raise the flaps and pushes it down to lower them. After either raising or lowering the flaps, it is customary to return the flap lever to a neutral position, midway between the up and down position, to relieve the pressure on the lines.

After lowering my flaps, I had returned the lever to this

neutral position. But I was not consciously focusing my attention on the act at the time, and consequently I failed to notice that I had overshot the neutral mid-position and, as a result, had retracted my flaps immediately after lowering them.

I hastily pushed the lever down as I crossed the boundary of the airport. The flaps extended again, in time to slow up my landing.

I have cited this case to show how we direct our attention to those things which are the most important to us. Previous to this incident, it had never occurred to me that one could make a mistake such as this which might cost him his life. Once I became aware that such a thing could happen, it became important to me to see that I did not make the same mistake again.

That is why we study and think: to organize our motivations so that we realize which ones are the important ones. If we rely on experience alone to make us realize which are the important ones, we may lose our life in the learning, as did another pilot I knew, who made the same mistake I made.

The teletype operator on the intermediate landing field at Delta, Utah, described this accident to me. The pilot was flying the identical type of attack bomber in which I had made the mistake I have described.

"First we heard from him," the teletype operator recalled, "he radioed us that one motor had quit over Milford, and that he was proceeding on one engine."

Apparently he failed to adjust his cross-feed.

"The next thing we heard from him," the teletype operator continued, "he was shouting, 'Mayday! Mayday!' "

Mayday is the SOS of the air. His other engine had failed him and he was preparing to bail out.

Apparently he remembered the cross-feed and adjusted it so that the good engine could draw from the tank that still contained fuel, for the next word heard from him was that he was continuing on one engine and intended to land at Delta. He gave his estimated time of arrival over Delta.

"He made a nice approach," said the teletype operator. "He put his gear down as he turned on the final approach and we saw his flaps extend when the airplane was about five hundred feet from the boundary of the field, and then retract again."

He had a clear approach on a runway 6100 feet long and was apparently doing a nice job of cool-headed flying, for, according to the teletype operator, "he crossed the approach end of the runway not over ten feet above the ground and did not seem to be traveling at an excessive rate of speed, but the airplane skimmed along just above the runway until he finally forced it down, just a few feet short of the runway's end. The plane slid across the end of the runway, beyond the boundary of the airport, into the rough sage-covered terrain, where it folded up like an accordion, fatally injuring the pilot."

It is evident that this pilot, with his mind engrossed with the problem of his single-engine landing, failed to direct his attention to the extending of his flaps. He performed this act as a sort of automatic reflex action and made the same mistake that I had made—unintentionally passing the mid-position when returning the flap lever to neutral and consequently retracting his flaps immediately after he had lowered them. He made this error under unfavorable circumstances and apparently never discovered the error.

Pilots who deny having made such obvious errors are not necessarily lying, for the memory is exceedingly unreliable concerning routine details performed in an automatic manner. Where such details can spell the difference between life and death, the pilot must learn to focus his attention upon them as he is performing the various acts, even though such acts are a part of an automatic routine.

This is an added reason for using the check-list. Not only will its use teach us to observe more closely, but on matters of vital importance we cannot afford to make a routine automatic check over the list, but must consciously check each detail so that we are sure. It is incredible how little time it takes to do this, since we switch our attention once the full awareness of a detail registers in the mind.

It is so important that the airplane pilot should be observant that we cannot overstress this vital point. You do not observe merely by staring intently at the scene before you. You observe when you know what you are looking for and switch your attention from one detail to another as quickly as you are sure you are fully aware of each detail.

We have placed stress on visual perception because it furnishes good examples, but the same principles apply with equal importance to all of our senses.

Since the airplane pilot is so dependent upon his visual perception, we will consider a few of the important principles which apply particularly to visual perception.

First of all, we will mention a little trick that will help you to cheat a little on your depth perception test when you take your physical examination for flying.

Move your head from side to side as you look at the two pegs, and your depth perception will become more accurate. The reason is that objects near the eye seem to move across the field of vision with respect to the more remote objects which seem to stand still. The brain interprets this phenomenon so that we see the stationary object as being farther away from us.

Your judgment of distance and your depth perception are both developed through your experience. The continual association of various phenomena with varying distances conditions the brain so that it automatically interprets such phenomena into terms of distance.

There are four clues of a similar character which aid in depth perception. These are clues provided through certain mechanical characteristics of the eye itself:

1. The clue we have mentioned, provided by moving the head from side to side. This clue will work equally well for a one-eyed person.

2. The clue furnished through the movements of the eye muscles in making accommodation for seeing objects at varying

distances. This clue does not depend upon bifocal vision.

3. The clue furnished by the muscles of the eye in converging the eyes upon an object. This clue depends upon bifocal vision.

4. The clue furnished by disparity: the fact that both eyes do not see exactly the same thing, or, to put it better, the image is not exactly the same in the retinas of both eyes. This clue depends upon bifocal vision.

Accommodation is of value as a clue to depth perception in distances up to two meters. As you know, we have an accommodation in vision for objects near the eye, within the two-meter range, and for objects in the distance. When people grow old, this accommodation loses its flexibility and they wear bifocal glasses: one lens which they look through for reading accommodates for near vision, and the other which they look through at distant objects accommodates for distant vision. In the younger person, the eye muscles change the lens of the eye to make this accommodation. The muscle movements that make accommodation possible provide a clue that is interpreted into distance by the brain but is of value only up to about two meters.

When you look at an object you would see double if the muscles of the two eyes did not cause the eyeballs to converge so that they focused on the same point. The nearer the object is to the eye, the more the eyeballs must be converged. This convergence is interpreted by the brain into a clue for distance. Beyond sixteen to twenty meters, there is so little convergence required that it becomes of little value.

If you place a cone against the wall some distance in front of you, so that the point or top of the cone is pointed directly toward you, and close the right eye, you will notice that you see more of the surface on the left side of the cone than you see on the right side. Similarly, if you close the left eye, you see more of the surface of the cone on the right side than on the left. In normal vision you see the well-balanced cone; the mind makes the adjustment for the disparity between what the two eyes see.

This adjustment also serves as a clue for depth perception since more adjustment must be made for objects nearer the eye.

This clue is of greater value the closer an object is to the eye, but there is no particular point at which it vanishes entirely, though it is of exceedingly little value when the distance of the object from the eye exceeds a mile, and it is of doubtful value at distances beyond 100 meters.

For all the value which is placed upon depth perception it becomes evident that, while it is an aid in judging distance, it is of doubtful accuracy except at distances relatively near the eye.

Our finest clues for the judging of distance are the comparisons of objects made by the mind itself. These comparisons are also conditioned by our experience.

At night, when we have no objects for comparison, or on an ocean or desert where there are relatively few objects available for comparison, we must fall back upon our depth perception. But, where objects are available for comparison, such comparisons are the most accurate of our clues for judging distance and are the ones we depend upon for most of our normal daytime judgment of distance, especially where any amount of distance is involved. Within the two-meter range we, of course, use these comparisons seldom if at all.

We also have four clues for comparison. These, incidentally, are the devices used so successfully by the artist in portraying distance in a picture that he paints.

1. The overlapping of objects: When one object overlaps another, the mind interprets the object that is partially obscured as being farther away. This is an infallible clue which cannot be misinterpreted. It is good at any distance and does not depend upon bifocal vision. In fact, none of these clues furnished by comparisons depends upon bifocal vision.

2. Linear perspective: The retinal image of an object decreases in size with distance, but our mind has been conditioned to make an adjustment for this, so that objects with which we are familiar, such as people, appear the same size regardless of the distance. A man does not appear as a pygmy in

the distance or as a giant when near at hand. This adjustment is interpreted into a judgment of distance by the eye.

The artist uses this device in drawing a railroad track. He draws the cross ties shorter and shorter and brings the lines that represent the rails closer together. We know that the cross ties are the same length and that the rails are spaced the same, so that this converging is interpreted to mean distance. This is the clue that we use most frequently and to the greatest profit—we don't always have overlapping objects.

3. Aerial perspective: Since we do not see objects that are far away as clearly as we do those that are near the eye, the mind interprets the haziness of objects to mean distance. The artist uses this sort of shading to portray distance too. This is a frequently used clue but can sometimes fool us. We know that people from the East, where the atmosphere is hazy and one cannot see far, are sometimes fooled by distances in the West, where one can see a great distance in the clear, dry atmosphere.

4. Shadows: Light normally falls on objects from above, so that shadows furnish some clues for distance. An extremely skillful artist uses these clues too, but it requires much more skill than do the other clues.

We have mentioned that linear perspective is the clue we use most frequently. We have pointed out that it is dependent upon the fact that the eye adjusts the diminishing size of an image on the retina to correspond to the true size of the object.

In vertical perception, that is, when looking up or down, the mind does not make such an adjustment. A man down on the street a few floors below you looks like a pygmy.

You remember we said that the mind was conditioned to accomplish this adjustment through experience. We have a great deal of experience in life in approaching and receding from objects. If we had never had such experience, we would not be able to judge distance. Since we have very little experience in approaching and receding from objects by means of ascent and descent, we have not developed this adjustment of size to distance in vertical perception.

You have seen the harvest moon when it looked as big as a balloon on the horizon and you know that a few hours later when it was directly overhead it appeared to be the size of a dime. You can prove that the retinal image of the moon is the same size in both instances by moving a penny out in front of the eye until it barely covers the moon. You will find that you hold the penny the same distance from the eye to cover the moon when it is directly overhead as when it is on the horizon.

Now look at the big moon on the horizon through a mailing tube that shuts out all near-by objects, and it will look the size of a dime the same as when overhead. Or look at it through a tiny hole in a piece of cardboard that shuts out near-by objects and it will appear to be the size of a dime.

Or look at that big harvest moon in a mirror, and again it will appear to be the size of a dime, as it does when it is overhead, demonstrating how the mind adjusts size to distance where it has experience to draw from. A man five hundred feet down the street appears to be man-sized, but, looking down at him from the top of a five-hundred-foot building, he appears to be a pygmy. In each case the retinal image was pygmy-sized, but in the first case your mind adjusted him to true size from its wealth of experience. With less experience in ascent and descent, the mind is less capable of making such an adjustment to size.

Look down or up at an object of considerable size, from a distance of a few hundred feet, and it appears to be tiny. Yet when viewed horizontally from the same distance, it appears to be its real size. This is the reason that so many airports appear to be the size of a postage stamp to the pilot looking down upon them. He must judge their size by comparison with surrounding objects. A field surrounded by city blocks and buildings will appear to be larger than it really is, whereas a field out in the desert or among the larger fields of prairie farm land will appear to be smaller than it is.

The pilot should guard against making tragic mistakes in estimating the size of airports and other objects that lie below him, for the mind does not automatically adjust distant objects to size in the vertical plane as it does in the horizontal plane. The pilot must carefully study the object, comparing it with objects with which he is familiar.

A Navy pilot had just been checked out on a heavy bomber of a type not too easy to fly. The field on which he checked out was rectangular so that the runway looked to be longer than it would have had it been on a square airport.

On his first cross-country flight with this heavy bomber, the pilot was to make his first landing on the Consolidated Airport, at Tucson, Arizona. This airport is a mile square, with runways as long as the runway on which this pilot had originally checked out. But this square airport appeared to be the size of a postage stamp, located as it was in the desert, and the runway on the square field looked exceedingly short. Davis-Mothan Airport, also at Tucson, Arizona, and but a few miles from Consolidated, is long and narrow, and the runway is really longer than the runways at Consolidated; it looked like Paradise by comparison.

The Navy pilot decided to land at Davis-Mothan, but the tower shooed him away, directing him to land at Consolidated. He made a half-hearted pass at Consolidated, but the runway looked so short to him that he overshot and returned to Davis-Mothan.

Just as he was leveling off to land, the tower again attempted to shoo him away and again directed him to land at Consolidated. He was nervous by this time; perhaps he was even a little frightened. He poured on the coal, without first trimming the airplane longitudinally for take-off.

The airplane was trimmed so tail-heavy for landing that with the application of full power for take-off the bomber shot up out of control and made a sort of cartwheel as it stalled, then crashed into the mess-hall. The bomber and its crew were destroyed, and the mess-hall burned.

Colors also make a difference in judging the size of an object. Assuming that the objects compared are of exactly the same size, a gray object will appear larger than a black object and a red object will appear larger than a gray object. If these factors were more generally understood, we might find artists who understand these principles rather useful in airport planning.

When I first opened my flying school I was using an exceedingly small airport surrounded by obstacles. In winter, when a near-by lake was frozen solid, I often used its almost limitless surface for a landing field. I was surprised to find that my students invariably had more difficulty with their landings on the vast expanse of the frozen lake than they did on the small, rough airport that was surrounded by obstacles.

I surmised that when coming in over a low fence they were able to judge when to level off, with the aid of the perspective furnished by the fence. I hauled a number of sawhorses down to the lake and built a low barrier for them to cross before landing. The results were amazingly good. I would take a student out to another part of the lake and find that he experienced difficulty in landing on the smooth expanse of ice. Then I would bring him over to the spot where I had constructed the low barrier and he would immediately make greatly improved landings.

On the other hand, a high barrier seems to present something of a mental hazard, and the results from such a barrier or obstruction are almost the opposite. I have found that by placing a low barrier out several hundred feet beyond the high barrier, so that the student uses the low barrier as a guide, much of this mental hazard of the high barrier is eliminated and the student's landings improve.

During World War II some gratifying experiments were conducted on some of the larger training fields, in which designs calculated to give the pilot some benefit from perspective were painted on the surface of the paved runways.

The ability to observe is highly important to the airplane pilot. To act without observing is like firing a gun without aiming it.

One can develop habits of observing by using the following rules:

1. Learn what to look for; then look for it. Make a checklist of those details that are important and consciously check each one.

2. Once you have seen what you are looking for, once you are fully aware of a detail, don't continue to stare, but switch your attention to the next detail.

It is important to understand how the mind fills in the gaps between the clues furnished by our sensory stimuli to complete the picture.

We are less likely to remember the things we see, hear, or feel in a routine automatic check than we are to remember the things that we consciously check.

Our background of experience is largely responsible for how we see, and how we make our judgments of distance and the size of objects—we learn to perceive. Such being the case, we can improve our perception by making an intelligent effort to do so.

# 7

# Developing the Reflexes

Steve Lacy and his navigator hurriedly swallowed their coffee and dashed out of the airport lunchroom to their flying gasoline tank. They were about to take off on a transcontinental non-stop race.

Their stubby airplane was practically a flying gas tank. The cockpit was so cramped that neither Steve nor his navigator wore a parachute.

The heavily loaded ship waddled slowly to flying speed, hanging to the ground as though plowing its way through sticky chewing gum.

Perilously near the far boundary of the field, the plane finally left the ground and began inching its way skyward. Steve was still climbing slowly when the first high slopes of the foothills of the Alleghenies loomed ahead. He had been nursing the motor with care, his eyes switching from the temperature gauges to the oil gauge, and then to the tachometer.

He had just finished checking his position with his navigator when some slight change in the tempo of the rhythmical roar of the motor caused him to glance quickly at the tachometer. Was it his imagination or had the motor lost a few rev's? The plane had ceased to climb, and the air speed was falling off; he had to nose down a bit. He noticed that the head-temperature was in the red.

There was but one thing to do. Mumbling a curse of disappointment Steve began a long, sweeping turn toward Roosevelt Field. The race was over as far as he was concerned.

The motor continued to lose power, and it soon became apparent that he would never reach Roosevelt Field unless he rid himself of the enormous load of reserve fuel. To attempt a forced landing in some field could end only in disaster with this heavy load of gasoline aboard—disaster in the form of a blazing wreck, fed by several hundred gallons of high octane gasoline.

The airplane was equipped with a dump valve by means of which the pilot could dump the fuel from the huge main gasoline tank located in the fuselage ahead of him. Steve leaned forward and pulled the lever which would dump the fuel.

The moment the gasoline began gushing out of the huge tank, Steve realized that someone at the factory had been guilty of a ghastly oversight. No hole had been cut beneath the dump valve, so that the gasoline could escape into the open air when the valve was opened; instead, it was filling the fuselage in which Steve and his navigator sat. Strong fumes of gasoline swirled about them. Soon the gasoline was an inch deep on the floor-boards, and Steve's heels were sloshing through the liquid as he operated the rudder controls.

Although gasoline was escaping from various holes and openings in the fuselage, it was not draining away fast enough to equal the flow from the dump valve. It was slowly inching up to Steve's ankles.

The fumes burned his nostrils and almost suffocated him. Roosevelt Field was just ahead of them now. He looked out at the wing which seemed bent and wavy, like a reflection in a crazy-house mirror. Over the nose, the front of the fuselage seemed to be bending too, as though the gasping motor were trying to bend its neck to turn around and leer at him.

Steve realized that his vision was rapidly deteriorating and might not last long enough to enable him to land. Somewhere he remembered having read that the sense of vision was the last of our senses to develop through the process of evolution, and the first one to leave us as we lose consciousness. He remembered taking ether when his adenoids and tonsils were to be removed; he recalled that long after his vision had failed he could hear voices that seemed to recede into the distance, growing farther and farther away, fainter and fainter, until all was void and blank.

This flash of insight gave Steve an idea. This gasoline . . . it was just like taking ether—it was putting him to sleep, and his

96

sense of vision was going first, just as it had with the ether.

His navigator, who was not compelled to remain in his seat deep down in the fuselage of the airplane, was sitting atop the rim of the cockpit so that the fumes did not seriously bother him. Steve shouted up to him, "I'm going blind! I'm afraid I won't be able to see to land. Keep telling me where we are, and how high we are, till we're on the ground, then roll off on the ground when the airplane slows up, just in case it explodes."

It seemed hopeless, but the navigator faithfully kept a steady stream of directions pouring into Steve's ears. By this time most of the gasoline had seeped out of the fuselage, but the deadly fumes were still there. As the plane crossed the boundary of the field, the navigator was shouting as loudly as he could into Steve's ears and shaking him by the shoulders, for Steve seemed to be in a coma, all but unconscious, but still flying like some automatic robot.

The navigator shouted his last instructions to Steve as the wheels struck the ground with a heavy thud and the airplane bounced high into the air. Steve made a masterful recovery, and the airplane settled and hung to the ground, rolling slowly to a stop, with Steve slumped unconscious over the controls.

It took a long time to revive Steve. He was never able to explain how he landed the airplane. "I was absolutely unconscious," he insisted. "The last thing I remember, was my navigator saying, 'Altitude fifty feet—airport two hundred feet ahead.' '

The navigator remarked that Steve was flying like a robot. As a matter of fact, that's about it—Steve had a well-developed set of conditioned reflexes which served as a robot.

I am sure that Steve's reflexes landed that airplane. He owed his life to the functioning of an auto-pilot within him —an auto-pilot that he himself had developed so that it could function with very little voluntary control from him. The reflexes are the last thing to cease functioning as we lose consciousness. The higher centers of Steve's nervous system had ceased to function, but the reflexes were not yet numbed. A few more seconds and perhaps they too would have ceased functioning, and the two men would have crashed to their deaths.

Steve had an exceptionally well-developed set of reflexes. He has entertained many an air-show audience by diving down, tapering out the dive so that at the bottom of the arc his wheels would touch the ground, then sweeping up into a slow easy loop, from the top of which he came screaming down in a graceful sweeping arc, at the bottom of which his wheels would just kiss the ground for a second time as he dropped a wing and wheeled up in a graceful climbing turn.

Steve would sit around an airport all day visiting with friends and then take off into the pitch-black night with his old Air King biplane that had no landing lights. To land in the darkness, he figured the location of his landing field from lights of automobiles on a highway and perhaps a few lighted farm houses. Then he glided in at a shallow enough angle so that when he contacted the ground the airplane would not crumple up or nose over but would simply bounce up into the air again. Steve had learned how to control this bounce so that he recovered from it settling down to the ground in a three-point landing position. He had done this so often that from the last fifty feet the landing was an automatic reflex act requiring no cerebral direction.

Every act we perform, all our skills, so essential to sports, the operation of mechanical devices, and the use of tools, depend upon the operation of these reflexes.

To begin with, we are born with a host of simple reflex movements that we do not have to learn, such as the patellar reflex, wherein our foot kicks up automatically when the knee-joint is tapped just below the knee-cap. These simple reflexes with which we are born permit us to make spasmodic, twitching movements, but to perform most of our activity we learn to assemble these movements and to time them.

Tickle a mule on its sensitive flank and the twitch of the skin is a simple reflex movement. But if the mule lets go with both feet and kicks you right through the side of the barn—that more complicated performance is a conditioned reflex activity which, unfortunately for you, the mule has learned.

The stimulation of certain receptors causes these reflex acts; thus certain receptors in the mouth are stimulated by the contact with food, the stimuli passing over a fixed pathway to evoke a flow of saliva. Now if some other stimuli are applied at the same time that the food contacts the mouth, for instance if a bell is rung each time a dog is fed, eventually saliva will drool from the dog's mouth when the bell is rung, even though there is no food present.

This is the fundamental principle of conditioning, which in more complex forms makes all of our learning possible.

It has been found that an animal can learn extremely simple conditioned reflex acts after the removal of the cerebral cortex, provided a powerful stimulus is applied over a long period of time. In the absence of the cerebral cortex a rabbit responds to such conditioning more readily than a decorticated dog, the dog in turn responding more readily than the decorticated monkey. From this it becomes apparent that in man virtually all of the learning or conditioning takes place in the cerebral cortex.

Through the process of learning we assemble and coordinate these simple reflex movements into more complicated acts, much as we assemble words, phrases, clauses, sentences, and paragraphs from the letters of the alphabet. We could not express our thoughts by the use of the letters of the alphabet alone, but, by assembling them into words, sentences, and paragraphs, there is no limit to the possibilities that we possess for expressing our thoughts.

These simple reflex acts which we do not have to learn, the simple movements that we are capable of making at the time we are born, are all obviously of service to the organism. You touch a hot stove and the simple reflex act that causes withdrawal of the finger serves to protect the finger from further injury.

Through the process of learning, we team these acts together and time them so as to produce a more complicated act that enables us to adjust to a new situation.

In the beginning, when we are babies, we learn accidentally through association. We accidentally team a couple of these reflex acts together and are pleased with the more complicated act; so we repeat it. Through such repetition, this more complicated act that we have learned to perform by the assembly of several simple reflex acts becomes automatic. We perform all the simple reflex acts which are a part of the more complicated act in an involuntary manner.

When you walk, your mind gives the order to walk and goes into none of the detailed acts which make walking possible, although you can, if you desire, exert voluntary control over some of the simpler parts of the act of walking. This you do in special circumstances, as on slippery ice, where you modify some of these simpler acts to adapt your manner of walking to the special circumstances.

Walking is a complex combination of many automatic reflex acts which were themselves built up from simple reflex acts, for we can combine and assemble these automatic reflex acts into still more complicated acts, almost without end. In fact, we have made so many such intricate combinations that most of our actions bear little resemblance to the original simple reflex acts of which they are composed. We are no more aware of the simple reflex acts than we are aware of the individual letters of the alphabet when we read.

How Do We Learn to Perform a Voluntary Act?

1. Our physiological drives, through our motivations, cause us to desire to do a certain thing. If this could be accomplished through the use of some automatic reflex action that we have already learned, we would use that action to carry out our motivation. But if no such automatic reflex act can do this we proceed to team together some of those at our disposal to accomplish our ends.

2. We could, and sometimes do, accomplish this by trial

and error. We team together some of the actions at our disposal, and the mind gives the order to act. If the response pleases us—good, we have succeeded. If not, we try another combination and still another, until we finally get the desired response.

3. The cerebral cortex has marvelous ability to make associations and, as the mind develops, we learn to think; we compare or associate past actions that we have made and plan for this new act we are about to make. In effect, we perform a lot of this trial and error in the cerebral cortex first. That's a lot quicker than trying it in physical action and saves a lot of wear and tear.

When out of these trial-and-error combinations the mind finds one that pleases it, one that we feel will work, we put the show on the road, we try it in our physical action. If the response pleases us—good, we have succeeded; if not, then we make some more associations to discover a combination that will work, or alter the combination that failed so that it will work. Then when we think we have it we try again, and again, until we finally succeed.

Much of this thinking is in itself automatic reflex activity of a more complicated nature taking place in the cerebral cortex. In the performance of most of our voluntary acts we are almost unaware of this process whereby the mind plans the act before we try it out physically, and the process is often accomplished with lightning speed.

If we are pleased with this new voluntary act that we have learned, we may repeat it again and again whenever the occasion demands, until it finally becomes an automatic reflex act that we can perform by simply willing it, without voluntarily directing the performance of the automatic acts of which it is composed, as we had to do when learning it.

It is as though we were born with a few, simple, mechanical parts at our disposal with which we could build some simple machines through assembling these simple parts in various combinations. Then we can combine these simple machines to build more complicated machines. There is almost no end to the combinations we can learn to make in this manner.

How Is the Automatic Reflex Developed?

1. We learn to perform the act voluntarily through the process just described. Many of our automatic reflexes develop automatically once we have discovered the combination that evokes the correct response, simply because the response pleases us and we repeat it whenever the occasion demands until it develops into an automatic reflex.

2. But suppose we do not wish to leave the development of this automatic reflex to chance. Suppose we wish to develop it quickly. How do we go about it?

We voluntarily repeat the act until we have weeded out all the incorrect responses that occasionally creep in. In this manner we develop technique. We've done the spade work; the lower centers of our nervous system complete the job.

3. In the lower centers of the nervous system, this automatic reflex is perfected. It is smoothed out until it is accomplished in an effortless, graceful style that we ordinarily call skill.

All needless reflex acts are eliminated. We built this new automatic reflex from existing automatic reflexes that we had at our disposal. Some of the reflex acts of which these are composed are not really essential in this new machine we have built. Hence the lower centers of the nervous system, through a process of conditioning of which we are not aware, weed out all these unnecessary motions, perfect the timing, and modify each act so that it is performed in just the proper strength. Once this conditioning has been accomplished, we perform the act gracefully and skillfully, with no conscious effort.

4. As long as we voluntarily control all the reflexes that make up the complete act, we do not allow the lower centers of the nervous system to carry out this process, since our cerebral cortex plays a dominant role in relation to the lower centers.

As we repeat the act, however, our attention is occasionally drawn to some other field. Whenever this happens, the lower centers of the nervous system take over the control of

102

the reflexes, until in time they are doing the whole job. The automatic reflex is fully developed, and we have simply to will the act to perform it. We need give no conscious effort to the details.

This tendency of the lower centers of the nervous system to take over gives us a clue for quickly developing the automatic reflex. We aid its development by directing our attention to definite limits within which the act is to be performed, thus allowing the lower centers to take over and smooth out the job we have started.

It may be easier to understand now why intellectuals often find it so difficult to develop grace and skill. They are unable to relinquish voluntary control over each act, and thus the development of the automatic reflex is retarded.

Let's see how a golf instructor helps the novice to develop this automatic reflex in learning how to drive a ball off the tee.

1. He shows the novice just how to grip the club, just how to stand, and the exact movements to be carried out in swinging the club.

The novice practices this combination of previously learned automatic reflexes until he gets the right response.

2. Then the instructor has him continue to practice until he has weeded out all the incorrect responses. Now he has the technique.

3. The instructor sets the ball on the tee and tells him to drive it out onto a spot ahead of him.

Do you see what the instructor has done? He has set some definite limits within which this act is to be carried out and encourages the novice to direct his attention to these limits. In so doing, the novice relinquishes some voluntary control over the individual steps of the technique and this favors the development of the automatic reflex.

4. Unfortunately, when the novice relinquishes voluntary control over the individual steps of the technique some incorrect responses may begin to creep in. So the instructor returns him to practicing the technique again until he has the proper response

and has weeded out all the incorrect responses. Then he again places the ball upon the tee and encourages the novice to perform the act within definite limits.

That is the correct manner for developing the automatic reflex act upon which all skills depend.

1. You learn to perform the act as a series or combination of other acts, practicing until you have the correct response and then continuing to practice until you have weeded out all the incorrect responses. That's technique.

2. Then you perform the act within limits so that your attention is drawn to the limits instead of to the individual acts that make up the complex action. This allows the lower centers of the nervous system to take over to smooth out and perfect the automatic reflex.

3. Whenever your technique suffers from lack of attention, whenever incorrect responses creep in, you withdraw your attention from the limits and again direct it to the series of the acts until you again have the proper technique.

Of course, each time you return to the perfecting of technique it takes you less time to go through the process.

You can, of course, supervise your own actions just as the golf instructor did, though such professional help is highly beneficial.

Some individuals rebel at the limits. They fail to realize that setting the limits actually causes the automatic reflex to develop more quickly.

It is as though we had designed an automatic machine that we could turn on and off at will. In decorticated animals it has been found that some of these automatic reflexes survive and that the animals need no further education for their performance. We can only assume that in such cases the act has become so fully automatic that it takes place as a more or less direct response to a characteristic pattern of stimuli, without any voluntary direction. If any voluntary direction is necessary to elicit the automatic reflex, then such a reflex will not survive in the decorticated animal.

What Advantages Are Gained Through the Development of These Automatic Reflexes?

Our mind is left free to solve other problems.

Muscular action is smoothed out in the lower centers of the brain, all unnecessary motion and movement being eliminated. You will notice that, as a man becomes skillful, he eliminates all unnecessary motion and movement and also applies no more force and strength to a movement than is essential, and that all the movements are perfectly timed to each other. His skill develops because the lower centers of the brain finish the job started by the cerebral cortex.

Now, the mind can take over voluntary control of this automatic reflex when it so desires, and for certain purposes it may occasionally make some variations to fit changing circumstances. Most of our activity is semi-voluntary.

It is interesting to note how one becomes awkward when he consciously tries to walk gracefully out on a stage before an audience, or when he tries to perform superbly on the dance floor, or to handle his eating tools with perfection at the banquet table. He loses the smooth grace of the automatic reflex when the mind voluntarily takes over the details.

When the instructor says that a student flies mechanically, he means that the student is performing each act voluntarily instead of letting the automatic reflexes take over. Not only does he place an extra burden upon the higher centers of the mind, making it difficult for him to learn the next step, but he performs his acts awkwardly, often applying more force than necessary and making many unnecessary movements.

At this point the value of a top-notch, capable instructor becomes evident. Such an instructor follows a program that not only enables the student to learn faster but develops precision flying habits at the same time.

Here is the program:

1. He demonstrates the maneuver with the student following through on the controls, to make sure that the student understands and will recognize the proper response when he

achieves it.

2. He has the student perform the maneuver until he gets the right response, then informs the student that he has the right response.

3. He has the student repeat the maneuver until all the wrong responses are weeded out, calling it to the student's attention when he makes a wrong response.

4. Once all the wrong responses have been weeded out, he establishes definite limits within which the maneuver must be carried out.

If the student is learning to fly straight and level, he has him hold a definite altitude, not only watching the position of the nose relative to the horizon but the altimeter as well. If the student is learning to turn, he has the student start and stop the turn at a definite point and maintain a definite rate of turn.

At any time that the student begins making wrong responses, his instructor immediately returns him to the beginning and takes him through the whole process again, but, as a rule, this is quickly accomplished and once the wrong responses are weeded out the instructor again lays down the limits within which the maneuver must be performed. He keeps at this until the student has satisfactorily established the automatic reflex.

The student, being required to perform the maneuver within definite limits, has his attention taken from the maneuver itself and directed to the limits, which for the moment is the important thing. This favors a condition in which the reflex will quickly become automatic.

The difficulty lies in the fact that, when the student directs his attention to the limits instead of to the maneuver itself, some undesirable responses often creep in, and the instructor must be patient, and on his toes as well, to return the student to the beginning step.

Admittedly, this is a disciplined method of instruction, which doesn't allow the student much time to "lollygog" around at the scenery.

Many students learn slowly because the instructor does not follow such a disciplined course of instruction but merely allows the student to fly around hit or miss until he accidentally develops some semblance of skill. Such students get so that they expect to go for a joy-ride instead of an instruction flight, and find it difficult to keep their attention on the problem at hand.

It is highly important that these automatic reflexes be properly developed. We might compare such reflexes to the auto-pilot with which most large military and air transport planes are equipped. The pilot sets up this auto-pilot by making the necessary adjustments so that it will fly the airplane. He then turns the flying of the airplane over to the auto-pilot and takes it easy, devoting his attention to the other details of flight.

If the pilot does not use care in setting up this auto-pilot, if he makes all the adjustments carelessly, then throughout the flight the auto-pilot will do a poor job of flying the airplane. This carelessness is lamentable when so little effort is required to adjust the auto-pilot properly.

The error in adjusting the auto-pilot may arise from inability of the pilot to be aware of the correct adjustment when he attains it, just as a student is sometimes not aware of the correct response when he gets it. Or the pilot may simply not give a damn. He may give it a slick and a dab and let it go as good enough. The student may also be too lazy to work until he has the response just right and may be willing to accept a response that is fairly close.

In establishing your automatic reflexes you are preparing for mass production, just as a manufacturer sets up jigs and makes patterns for mass production. If the jigs and patterns are not right, then each product that comes off the assembly line will have a defect. If you do not develop your reflexes properly in the beginning, you will fly sloppily as long as you fly, unless you decide to relearn, which means unlearning bad habits and substituting new, correct ones. This process is much more difficult than learning properly in the first place.

The effective method for developing an automatic reflex will bear repetition:

1. Practice until you have attained the desired response.

2. Continue to practice until you have weeded out all undesirable responses.

3. Then set definite limits within which the act must be performed.

4. Any time an undesired response creeps in, go back and start all over from the beginning.

# 8
# Learning to Coordinate

I once knew a couple of mechanically inclined boys who pooled their resources and bought a cracked-up airplane, which they rebuilt. It took more money to complete the job than they had anticipated. When the airplane was ready to fly, they lacked money for flying lessons.

They had read numerous books on how to fly and had a fair understanding of the essentials of flying, save perhaps the psychological factors. They again decided to pool their resources and fly as a team, each one taking over half of the job. One would handle the control stick while the other handled the rudder and throttle.

Pooling their resources didn't work out so well in flight, as it had in the rebuilding of the airplane. Fortunately the two boys survived this co-operative venture, but the airplane did not.

Flying requires a considerable amount of co-ordination. This means that the various simple acts that make up the more complex actions essential to flying must be timed to each other, and each performed in strength to harmonize with the total situation. There must be a correct adaptation of parts, one to another, so as to form a connected whole.

Actually, co-ordination, as we use the term in flying, is just another automatic reflex act built up or assembled from other automatic reflex acts, the main distinction being that the timing and the relative strength with which the various parts of the complex act are performed are the features most difficult to achieve. It is not enough to assemble a series of movements into a complex act; they must be timed and each must be performed in proper strength.

Watch an inexperienced person getting into a canoe. He may perform all the various acts essential to getting safely into the boat but he does not properly adapt these acts to one another.

One must know all the essential movements which enter into any complex action or maneuver before he can make any serious attempt to co-ordinate them. Often a lack of coordination may stem from a lack of such knowledge.

To master co-ordination one should analyze the maneuver. In making a turn, for instance, the flier applies rudder in the direction in which he wishes to turn, at the same time depressing the wing which will be on the inside of the turn. He does this to initiate the turn. When he has attained the desired rate of turn, he returns the rudder to its normal central position, and when the desired rate of bank has been established, he maintains just enough pressure on the controls, in the direction of the high wing, to prevent overbanking. The airplane is maintained in the turn by a slight back pressure on the elevator controls, just as a rock tied to a string, which you swing in a circle around your head, is maintained in its turn by the string which you hold in your hand. If you ease out on the string, the radius of turn increases, while if you pull in on the string, the radius of turn decreases.

Once the rate of turn has been established, the airplane is maintained in the turn by the fore and aft pressure applied to the elevator controls, back pressure being increased to tighten the turn and eased off to widen the radius of the turn. The angle of bank must be kept in the proper proportion to the rate of turn or the nose will rise or drop.

Students who do not understand these principles will, of course, endeavor to maintain a uniform rate of turn by continually jockeying the rudder and will endeavor to hold the nose in the proper relation to the horizon by the use of the elevator control.

In many cases, motor torque has such a bearing on the problem that the student finds the maneuver difficult to grasp. For instance, an old Avro with a rotary motor had so much motor torque that it would turn to the left on a dime with a nickel left over but needed all outdoors for a right turn. As a result of motor torque, the nose tends to descend when entering a left turn and to rise when entering a right turn and, in similar fashion, to rise when recovering from a left turn and to descend when recovering from a right turn.

This motor torque effect to some extent substitutes for back pressure on the controls when entering a right turn. In shallow turns it may sometimes even be necessary to maintain a little forward pressure on the elevators when entering a right turn, to counteract the effects of motor torque.

The student finds it easier to turn to the left, since in this case he is always applying a normal back pressure on the elevator controls and finds it easier to maintain the correct rate of turn. Some pilots even develop into what are known as "left-hand pilots," preferring to execute all maneuvers to the left.

After mastering these facts the student is ready to learn to co-ordinate. He finds that the proportion of pressure applied in holding off bank bears a relation to the proportion of back pressure he will apply to the elevator control. Thus if he wishes to make a climbing turn, he finds that he is applying more pressure toward the high wing to hold off bank, otherwise the increased back pressure on the elevators would merely tighten the turn.

If he wishes to make a nosed-down, spiraling turn, he discovers that as he releases some of the back pressure on the elevator controls he also applies less pressure toward the high wing.

When a student has difficulty in mastering co-ordination in turns, many instructors let him make a few gliding turns with power off, since such turns are much easier to co-ordinate because of the absence of motor torque.

A student experiencing difficulty in coordinating his turns will also find it easier if the instructor trims the airplane so that it is nose-heavy, since the student will then find it necessary to apply considerable back pressure on the elevator controls, even in right-hand turns.

Students should be started on turns of thirty to forty

degrees of bank, since a fairly steep turn is easier to coordinate than a shallow turn. Some instructors insist on starting the student on shallow turns which are the most difficult turns to co-ordinate, with the possible exception of the vertically banked turn.

The application of aileron and rudder when entering the turn, the pressure to use on the elevators to maintain the correct rate of turn, and the application of rudder and aileron when recovering from the turn, all must be timed to each other and the proper portion of pressure used in their application.

Exactly the same procedure is used as in mastering any automatic reflex act.

1. The instructor demonstrates the maneuver with the student following through on the controls so that the student gets some idea of the timing and application of pressure desired.

2. The student practices until he gets the right applications of pressure and the proper timing.

3. The student continues to practice until he has weeded out all incorrect timing and all incorrect applications of pressure.

4. The instructor requires that the maneuver be performed within definite limits, thus directing the student's attention to the limits rather than to the maneuver itself, a condition favorable for the reflexes to take over and become automatic.

5. When any incorrect responses creep in, the instructor takes the student back to begin all over again.

To develop co-ordination in turns, such devices as figure-eights around pylons, co-ordination exercises, wing-overs, and split-S turns are used.

In using all such devices it is important that the student should be required to stay within or adhere to limits. He must use the pylons for reference points or, in the case of coordination exercises, wing-overs, and split-S turns, he may use a paved highway or fence line for reference. The wing-overs and split-S turns may also be executed around pylons.

In developing the timing so essential to proper co-ordination, anticipation is a potent factor. Thus when a student levels off from either a climb or a glide, he must anticipate the point at which the leveling off must begin or he will overshoot his mark and waver up and down in a bracketing process until the desired level has been attained.

Leveling off plays such an important part in landing that a student will find landings exceedingly difficult until he learns how to level off without too much of this bracketing. Unless he can learn to anticipate the moment at which he should begin leveling off for the landing, he will run into much the same trouble that I experienced on my two parachute jumps—my first and last—accomplished simultaneously.

I did not anticipate the moment of contact with the ground correctly, with the result that I cushioned my fall with the customary reflex actions too soon and struck the ground in an awkward position. I found it necessary to take my next few meals standing up.

Much of this co-ordination seems to be accomplished in the pathways of the lower centers of the brain. Thus one's flying is not likely to smooth out until the automatic reflexes take over. Requiring the student to perform all maneuvers within definite limitations encourages the automatic reflexes to take over, by diverting the student's attention to the limits or, rather, to the problem of staying within the limits.

It is understandable that students are likely to take the attitude that the important thing is to make a smooth, coordinated turn, wing-over, or other maneuver. In that assumption they are being logical, but it is not logical to believe that it is not important to hold to the pylon, the railroad track, the fence line, or whatever reference medium is being used.

Holding to the pylon or reference line directs the student's attention to the limits within which the maneuver is to be executed rather than to the individual motions involved in that particular maneuver, thus leaving the lower centers of the nervous system free to smooth out and time those individual motions into smooth, coordinated action.

Adhering to definite limits—holding to pylons and reference lines—seems to complicate the problem unnecessarily, but actually such a procedure fosters a quick development of smooth, coordinated flying.

It is, of course, necessary that the student learn the technique of the maneuver before he begins performing the maneuver within definite limits.

Practicing technique alone in an effort to develop coordinated action, without setting limits within which that maneuver is to be executed, is one of the common faults that leads to mechanical flying. When the student performs the maneuver within definite limits, he develops two highly desirable flying qualities for the price in effort of developing one. He develops co-ordination and precision flying habits at the same time.

Around crowded airports, in heavy traffic, precision flying is essential. It is necessary in instrument flying. It is required in military flying, and all the tests which the candidate must perform on his flight check for his pilot's license are based on his ability to fly precisely.

Precision flying should not be regarded as a final polishing-off process, but should be learned as each new automatic reflex is developed, right from the first lesson.

The idea of the sky as a limitless medium, in which one may wallow sloppily around as he pleases, where he may act only when and howsoever he feels like acting, where he may be as free as the birds, where, in short, he may enjoy complete undisciplined freedom with no encroaching barriers; all this may indeed seem like a lovely road. But it is a road which may lead to disaster and is certainly not likely to lead one to become a capable pilot. To enjoy his freedom, man must learn to set and to stay within his own limits; he must learn to control himself.

Much the same principles apply to self-control as apply to the control of the airplane. One does not drive an airplane; he lets the airplane fly itself, acting only to maintain it within certain limits.

After a student, on his first lesson, has whipped an airplane all over the sky in an attempt to drive it, the instructor may say, "Now turn loose of the controls and see how much better the airplane flies itself."

You decide on the limits within which you are going to keep the airplane and make no movement of the controls until the airplane approaches one of these limits. Then you make a decisive movement, calculated to restore it to a place safely between those limits. By "decisive" we do not mean a heavy or violent application of pressure to the controls. The slightest pressure may under certain conditions be a decisive movement, for a decisive movement is for a definite purpose, performed in such a manner as to achieve that purpose, and stopping right there.

One becomes skillful by eliminating all waste motion, useless tension, and the expenditure of unnecessary energy when performing an act.

Go to the beach and watch swimmers. Which ones make the most effort, the skilled swimmers or the beginners? Make the same observations on the dance floor, or watch artisans in the performance of any skill.

If you stand behind an airline pilot while he is making an instrument let-down, you will be amazed at the few movements he makes, especially if you are aware of the tremendous number of details to be attended to during such a let-down.

Now climb into a Cub with an inexperienced pilot. If your seat has a set of dual controls in front of it, you may feel like drawing your knees up onto the seat to prevent their being battered by the wild movements of the control stick as it lashes back and forth around the cockpit, and at the same time you will notice that the pilot is doing anything but precision flying.

It seems unbelievable but it is a fact that precision flying requires much less effort than sloppy flying. What is even more unbelievable is that one can learn precision flying more rapidly than sloppy flying, since setting of definite limits tends to encourage the automatic reflexes to take over.

Precision flying simply means that you set certain limits and then make an effort to stay within those limits. It means that you make no movements of the controls except when such a movement is necessary to keep the airplane within the limits. It means that you fly the airplane, instead of letting the airplane fly you. It means that you plan each maneuver and stick to your plan. When you make a turn you know at what point you are going to start the turn, at what rate you will turn, and at what point you will recover or come out of the turn.

No pilot can possibly avoid certain situations where he must keep the control of the airplane within certain definite limits. The precision pilot does not have to put forth any special effort upon such an occasion. With his automatic reflexes doing the work of flying, his mind is free to deal with more intricate special problems related to the flight.

How different this is from the pilot who flies sloppily. When he finds himself in a critical situation, he must devote almost all of his attention to precision flying and has little attention available for other vital matters.

His movements of the controls will be harsh and awkward —"mechanical" is the word—and he will be tense, with perspiration oozing from his pores. Is it any wonder that he so often fails in critical situations?

To sum up: Those smooth, graceful, well-timed movements with which any skill is performed are due largely to the development of pathways in the lower centers of the brain, and they can be developed through practice only.

Definite limits should be set when practicing, so that the attention is directed to conforming to those limits. This favors the development of any automatic reflex once the correct response has been achieved and the incorrect responses have been weeded out.

# 9

# The Building of Confidence

You go into a strange restaurant to eat. You hang your hat on a hook on the wall, then sit down at a table some thirty feet away, with your back to your hat. You cannot rely on the integrity of the restaurant owner. You do not trust the people about you.

Every few seconds you turn and look to reassure yourself that your hat is still there. On one of these occasions you accidentally upset a bowl of hot soup in your lap. Eventually, you dribble jelly on your new tie, and finally you spill your coffee. It hasn't been a very agreeable meal.

This is a fair example of the type of behavior that a lack of confidence produces. When you lack confidence, you continually examine the future in an effort to reassure yourself. You are continually estimating and re-estimating your chances for success or, perhaps more truthfully, the likelihood of disaster.

More of your attention is occupied by these estimates of the likelihood of failure than is directed to the problem at hand. Is it any wonder that lack of confidence breeds failure?

The emotions of the confident man flow more smoothly. His mental processes function at a faster rate and, to top it off, he has a delightful feeling of well-being.

There is no magic word or thought that can bring you confidence. You can't just will yourself into being confident.

In fact, an attempt to do so seems to make one even less confident.

A man approached Moody, the great evangelist, and said, "I would like to be a Christian but I just can't make myself believe. What can I do to become a Christian?"

Quick as a flash, Moody replied, "Start acting like a Christian and the first thing you know you'll be one."

If one behaves like a confident man behaves, he stands a good chance to gain confidence.

Here is how a confident person behaves:

1. He trusts his own capabilities.

2. He relies on himself to work out his problems.

3. He holds his attention to the problem at hand until a solution is achieved and then moves on to the next problem. He keeps an over-all picture of the entire problem in his mind, but refrains from worrying about future steps of the problem until those steps are at hand, leaving his mind free to deal with the immediate step at hand. He does not continually inventory and then re-inventory his possibilities for success. He takes it for granted that he will succeed and, on that assumption, solves each step in turn. He possesses confidence, which is a feeling that he has the capacity and ability to accomplish a given task.

Suppose we do not have this feeling of well-being, such as the confident person has, this feeling that we can and will succeed? In that event, though we do not admit it, our decision to go ahead is not final. Though we may not be conscious or aware of it we are still considering giving up. We continually speculate on the possibility of failure.

In effect, we have two goals: one, to go ahead, the other, to give up, and this latter goal takes so much of our attention that we are likely to fail.

Sometimes we can bolster our confidence by simply refusing to contemplate or speculate on failure. In making long flights over water, there is a "point of no return," so called because once this point has been passed the pilot has used so much fuel that he has lost the option of turning back. Many pilots have told me that they felt better and that their confidence increased immeasurably, once they had passed the point of no return.

In like manner we often find that our confidence increases when we become irrevocably committed to a definite course of action. If we are going to go ahead, there is no sense in continually speculating on our chances of failure. The smart thing to do is either to give up and do nothing or to go ahead on the assumption that we are going to succeed.

Our fear of the unknown is always greater than our fear of the known. Noises may frighten us in a dark warehouse until we turn on the lights. The future is dim as compared with the present. We cannot see into it too well—hence, the terrible forebodings.

Sometimes it is even a relief when disaster finally strikes, because the uncertainty of the possibilities that the future seemed to hold was worse than the effects of the disaster itself.

Confidence is a reaction to success just as lack of confidence is a reaction to failure. Confidence is built upon accomplishment. Once you stay on a bicycle for a block, you know you can ride a bicycle. Once you have succeeded in swimming a few strokes, you know you can swim.

Lack of confidence is built upon failure. Hence, to prevent a lack of confidence we should avoid failure as much as possible. One way of doing this is to persist in what we attempt to do until we are able to quit with the taste of success in our mouths. That is the reason it has been considered wise to send a pilot right up on another flight following an accident; the idea of failure will not then linger in his mind.

Failure does not cause a great loss of confidence in some individuals, largely because of the attitude they take toward it. It seems that they analyze their failures, possibly without realizing it.

A. They determine the reason for their failure.

B. They devise plans for preventing a similar failure in the future.

1. They may prepare themselves better, develop greater skill, or acquire more knowledge.

2. They may break down the problem into easy steps, each one of which they feel confident they can accomplish. Such a plan gives them confidence for the future.

Other individuals alibi: "It was fate," "The world is against me," or "People try to make me fail." It is with such individuals that failure produces such a devastating loss of confidence; they feel they cannot succeed. When one places the blame for failure upon his own methods in attacking the problem, he leaves an avenue open for success in the future through changing those methods. When one blames fate for his failure, he leaves no such avenue open.

Since it takes success to breed confidence, we are wise if we place ourselves in a position where we can succeed, either by breaking down the problem into easier steps or by lowering our sights a trifle.

The wise instructor builds confidence in a student by continually placing him in positions where he can scarcely fail to succeed, moving him ahead in such easy steps that he enjoys a continual series of successes.

Give a horse too heavy a load—a load that it cannot possibly move—and you are likely to have a balky horse on your hands. You can make a balky horse out of the finest thoroughbred, by continually giving it loads that it cannot budge.

That is just about what a man who lacks confidence is—a balky horse.

You have watched a balky horse; it goes through all the motions, but it doesn't get down and lay-in to-the-harness and pull.

A person who lacks confidence goes through all the motions, but he doesn't work with all his capabilities and energies. He is indecisive—like the balky horse, he holds back. It is this indecisive action that makes a lack of confidence apparent.

There is great truth in the old adage, "Nothing succeeds like success." Success produces confidence, and with confidence we go ahead to greater success. It is a cumulative, progressive situation.

Unfortunately, the opposite can also be true. With failure we lose confidence and sink to deeper and deeper depths. Such a condition can become chronic; then it becomes known as a state of depression.

We find a state similar to depression in an animal when it emerges badly wounded from mortal combat with its torn flesh bleeding, or when it falls over a cliff or meets with some other accident that leaves its body bruised and broken. Under such circumstances further action cannot be effective; shock and the parasympathetic emotion of resignation take over to regulate the normal processes by which the strength of the animal may be conserved and restored. The animal will crawl away into some deep thicket or dark cave, where it will lie for days, inert, almost like dead, while the mending processes of nature proceed. This is an adaptive reaction, since any effort would weaken the animal still further and lessen its chances of recovery.

During this state engendered by the parasympathetic emotion of resignation, the mental processes have slowed, the nervous system is working at a retarded rate, and it will take extremely strong stimuli to arouse any response in the animal.

When a human being meets with continual failure, or when he is struck with some terrible disaster, when a friend on whom he depends is taken from him by death, when he fails in business, when he does not feel that he can go on, when any tragedy, either real or imagined, strikes him, when he feels that he cannot act effectively, this same parasympa-thetic emotion of resignation takes over to conserve and restore his strength.

The emotion of resignation is not always in keeping, however, with the conditions of reality. He may still possess the strength and power for effective action and it may be highly essential that he should act, but under the influence of this parasympathetic emotion of resignation he remains inert and passive.

Such a condition may be relieved by various sympatho-mimetic drugs that stimulate the central nervous system, thus speeding the mental processes. Strangely enough, it has been demonstrated that such drugs actually give one a feeling of confidence with no impairment of judgment.

The parasympathetic emotions act as a sedative to lull one away from action. They have their place in life, just as sedatives have their place in medicine, but when one needs to act effectively he should not take a sedative; nor can he expect to act effectively when depressed by emotion.

If a person takes an overdose of sleeping pills, or some other sedative or narcotic drug, and a physician is called in, what does the physician do? He immediately administers some powerful sympathomimetic drug such as Adrenalin or Benzedrine Sulphate, which counteracts the effects of the sedative by speeding up the mental processes. In the hands of a competent physician, these same sympathomimetic drugs are used to relieve depression, in exactly the same manner, by speeding the mental processes.

In like manner, our sympathetic emotions enrich the blood with two sympathomimetic drugs. One is sympathin and is produced at the ends of the sympathetic nerves when they are stimulated. Minute amounts find their way into the blood stream. The other, adrenin, is produced by the medulla of the adrenal glands when those glands are stimulated by a sympathetic emotion. Hence our sympathetic emotions speed up our mental processes.

Elation is the sympathetic emotion which underlies confidence. Elation seems designed to cause us to strike while the iron is hot, to follow a weakening of the foe with the kill. It is the emotion that drives us to further action when things are coming our way. If we experienced a feeling of peace and contentment when we saw our foe weakening, or when we saw a solution to our problem, we would relax and fail to deliver the "coup de grace" which makes action effective.

This speeding of the mental processes is but one of the two outstanding physical characteristics that accompany confidence.

Confidence also releases us from the inhibitions that restrain our actions. That is why we lay-into-the-harness and pull when we have confidence, and why, when we lack confidence, we act indecisively, held back by our inhibitions.

The higher centers of the nervous system inhibit reflex activity. You see this confirmed when you chop a chicken's head off and it tumbles about with all its reflexes functioning at full speed.

All of our sympathetic emotions speed the mental processes, but each one releases us from a certain set of inhibitions. This feature is that which distinguishes and characterizes our various sympathetic emotions. For instance, most of us possess certain inhibitions that prevent us from striking a fellow being, but anger releases these inhibitions and we are likely to punch someone in the nose when we are angry.

Most of us possess certain inhibitions that hold us from running during a time of danger, but fear releases us from these inhibitions and we get going—but quick.

Most of us possess inhibitions that hold us back from peeping through keyholes, but curiosity releases us from these inhibitions and we glue our eye to the keyhole.

Most of us possess inhibitions that make us wary, that cause us to proceed with caution lest we make a mistake. But elation releases us from these inhibitions and we act with confidence.

We experience a feeling of well-being when released from our inhibitions.

We know that some sedative drugs do seem to produce a feeling of confidence despite the fact that they slow the mental activities. The explanation is that they first numb the top centers of the nervous system, the cerebral cortex, thus removing our inhibitions and giving us that characteristic feeling of well being that accompanies confidence.

Suppose we consider a widely used sedative with which many of us may be familiar—alcohol. Any doctor will tell you that alcohol is a sedative, despite the apparently stimulating effects that result from a release of our inhibitions.

If you still doubt that alcohol is an anesthetic, the discovery made by Samuel Guthrie in the year 1831 should convince you.

Here is the formula that he used for making what he called a superior brand of sweet whiskey: Into a clean copper still, put three pounds of chloride of lime and two gallons of good whiskey. Distill, watching the process carefully so that, when the product ceases to be highly sweet and aromatic, it can be removed and tightly corked.

Guthrie recommended his product highly as being vastly superior to ordinary whiskey. It tasted better and produced far more potent results. He would often give a bottle of this sweet whiskey to his friends when they wanted to celebrate a bit. Today this same sweet whiskey of Samuel Guthrie's is known as chloroform.

Through numbing the cerebral cortex, alcohol relieves our inhibitions; we have a simulated feeling of well-being, as a result of this release from our inhibitions.

We do possess this one characteristic of confidence—a release from our inhibitions to action—but we lack the other characteristic, the rapidly functioning mental faculties. Furthermore, this feeling of false confidence is accompanied by an impairment of our sense of values and of judgment. We may act when under the influence of alcohol, but our actions are not likely to be effective and are likely to be of such a nature as to get us into a lot of trouble.

Some people seem just naturally to possess few inhibitions. They exhibit a sort of bravado which is somewhat akin to confidence. It is not based on successful performance but upon a mild mental deficiency.

True confidence is based upon success or upon a process of logical reasoning by means of which we have convinced ourselves that we have devised a plan for action that will bring success. It is accompanied by the following characteristics that favor effective action:

1. Release from those inhibitions that cause us to be wary and indecisive.

2. A speeding of the mental processes.

This feeling of confidence arises when we encounter conditions that we have met successfully in the past or when we devise a plan for action based upon what we consider logical reasoning.

Elation is a sympathetic emotion that produces much the same effects as a sympathomimetic drug. It causes the mental processes to speed up. It causes the heart to beat faster. It increases the rate of respiration. It causes the blood to be enriched with sugar. It prepares man to put forth a supreme effort to deliver the "coup de grace" that crowns effective action.

The emotion of elation is learned or conditioned. From our past experience we learn that under certain conditions we can expect to succeed.

If we take the viewpoint that we are unlucky and that fate is against us, we are not likely to recognize any conditions under which it is likely that we shall succeed. On the other hand, if we see how, by changing our methods of attack, we can succeed under conditions where we have previously failed, it is possible that we may even feel elation when we recognize these conditions under which we previously failed, for now we also recognize that we can turn these same conditions to our own good.

Religious faith gives many people confidence. I do not mean a profession of faith—but real faith. Such an individual does the best he can. He keeps his mind on the problem at hand, secure in his faith that God expects of him only that he should put forth his best effort; win or lose he will have succeeded in pleasing God if he does his best with the talents with which he is endowed. His elation comes from the belief that he is pleasing God—that, for him, is success. He does not speculate overly much on the possibilities of failure—he simply does his best and leaves the outcome in the hands of God.

Friends upon whom you can rely also foster confidence, as well as a feeling of elation which comes from the realization that they will help you to succeed—that their strength is your strength.

Hundreds of inspirational books have been written extolling various devices for lifting the depressed soul to the heights of elation, but the surest way to develop confidence is to cultivate success, since confidence is the feeling that we can and will succeed.

You can develop confidence by:

1. Making sure you can accomplish what you attempt, either by breaking down the problem into easy steps, by giving yourself greater preparation, or, if these fail, by lowering your sights a trifle, so that your ambitions are consistent with your abilities.

2. Analyzing your failures to determine why you failed and then making plans whereby you can change your method of attack, so that you may succeed next time.

You can breed lack of confidence by:

1. Biting off more than you can chew and then giving up before you have put forth your best effort.

2. Rationalizing your failures—"Fate is against me." "I'm just naturally unlucky." "People don't want me to succeed." And worst of all: "I'm not competent and can never become competent—I'm handicapped."

3. A refusal to recognize reality, and depending upon luck or coincidence rather than your own efforts to solve a problem. When you realize that the solution of a problem depends upon your own efforts, you will understand that capabilities must match ambitions, that you must either increase your capabilities or reduce your ambitions to make the two consistent, as they must be for effective action and success.

When you have failed, you can regain confidence by perfecting a plan that you know will bring success in the future. Bemoaning your bad luck will only weaken your confidence.

Confident action is action based on the belief that you are going to succeed. To speculate on the possibilities of failure weakens your confidence.

All possibilities for failure should be carefully considered when you make your plans, so that you will be prepared to circumvent them. But once you begin acting upon your plan, these speculations as to the possibilities for failure should be forgotten and you should lay-into-the-harness, knowing that your actions are going to be effective.

I do not mean that you should ignore reality—we cannot afford to do that. If you are a skillful planner, you will have made alternate plans to which you can switch at any time your first plan fails.

The flight plan of an airplane pilot furnishes a good example of this. A pilot clears for the Los Angeles Air Terminal, but with an alternate at Palmdale. If Los Angeles is shrouded with fog upon his arrival, he will switch to his alternate plan and proceed to Palmdale.

In fact, possession of an alternate plan, in case we meet with insurmountable obstacles in carrying out our original plan, gives us an added feeling of security.

Determination helps, for you are less likely to speculate upon the possibility of failure if you are determined to succeed.

Confidence is not a gift from the gods. It is within your reach and mine. We develop it through intelligent planning followed by determined intelligent effort. It is the crowning glory of success and beckons us on to still greater success.

# 10

# The Building of Judgment

There are two kinds of judgment—good and bad. We must not overlook the fact, however, that there are those who seem to possess little or no judgment. These are the people who play hunches or flip a coin. As a rule, their flying careers are rather short.

Whenever we have more than one course of action open to us, we are called upon to render a decision, to use our judgment. We cannot do better than to adopt the methods used in court procedure in making our judgments.

In rendering a decision, a judge goes through the following procedure:

1. He listens to the evidence. In your case, you observe and gather the data which form your evidence.

2. He excludes all irrelevant evidence.

3. He weighs the evidence; he decides the relative importance of the various bits of data.

4. He makes his decision.

5. That decision stands, unless new data or evidence is made available, or unless it can be shown that the judge was prejudiced by personal factors when he made his decision.

Getting the Evidence

Many poor judgments result from a failure to get sufficient evidence. We need all the important data before we make our decision.

Joe Jukes was flying a Swallow biplane equipped with a 225 h.p. motor. He landed in a forty-acre field in which a heavy stand of clover was about ready to be cut for hay. Since he knew that the airplane could get off in about half the distance to the fence, he gave her the gun and away he went. He knocked down quite a bit of good, strong fence and tore off the landing gear and the two lower wing panels, because he had failed to gather all the data.

Had he noted that there was a dead calm at the time; had he remembered that his altimeter showed 500 feet above the ground that morning before he had adjusted it back to zero; and, most important of all, had he considered how the tall clover would make it difficult for him to gain speed for the take-off, I do not believe he would have tried to take off without first having a strip of clover mowed.

The light air, the absence of any wind to assist his take-off, and the tall clover, all were overlooked in making his decision. He almost cleared the fence.

Irrelevant Data

Too often a pilot lets irrelevant data, which should not influence him, to creep into his decisions.

One morning in mid-winter, following a heavy snow, a salesman who was employed by my school suggested that I allow him to take one of our trainers and fly to a town some forty miles away to interview a prospective student. I pointed out that this town had no airport and that the snow was too deep in the open fields for a safe take-off.

When I returned from a business engagement in town, I found that he had disregarded my advice and had taken one of my training planes and was on his way.

Darkness settled over the airport, and he had not returned. About ten o'clock that night the telephone rang, and my salesman gave me the sad news.

It seems that he had learned that a salesman from a rival school was driving up to see the same prospect, and he decided to beat his rival to the punch by flying. He succeeded in this part of his venture but was not so successful in his attempt to take off. He must have realized after the first attempt that the snow was so deep that he could not get off. But I suppose he was afraid that I would say, "I told you so!"

He taxied back and forth across the field a dozen times before he finally gave up. But his defeat was only temporary. He got a man to come in with a road grader and clear a runway for him. Then he was ready for the final attempt.

While taxiing back and forth across the field, the snow that had blown in through a hole beneath the controls had collected in the fuselage. Snow filled the cockpit, level with the seat rails. There must have been a couple of hundred pounds packed into the rear of the fuselage.

The airplane finally wobbled off the ground with the tail dragging, shot up into the air, and cart wheeled over on one wing, then over on its back. All it needed in the way of repairs was a new fuselage and four new wing panels. Since the airplane landed on its back, the under-carriage escaped injury.

The salesman's anxiety to get to the prospect was irrelevant and not a part of the data which should have influenced his decision. Just because we desire to do something does not guarantee the success of an action one iota. The fear that I might criticize him was still more irrelevant. The critical opinions of others do not influence the success of a venture one iota either. Yet, how frequently we base our decisions on such irrelevant data.

Weighing the Evidence

In comparing the data, one must be careful not to give too much importance to minor bits of evidence. A common weakness in judgment lies in a faulty weighing of the evidence. You are familiar with the simple, old type of balance scales which the blindfolded lady holds in her hands in the familiar scene that depicts justice. The object to be weighed is placed in one pan, and weights to balance it are placed in the other pan.

Before you can do a good job of weighing the evidence, you must organize the evidence. When one fails to organize and weigh the evidence, his judgment is likely to carry about the same value as a shrewd guess, and most of us like to make a second, sometimes a third, and possibly a fourth guess.

Suppose there was a prize for guessing the number of beans in a quart jar in a store window. If you made a guess of, say, 10,000 beans, you might very likely wish to change this guess the next day, especially if the prizes were very attractive.

Suppose, however, you went home and got some beans which by careful comparison seemed to be the same size as the beans in the jar. Then you found a receptacle which would hold exactly one cubic inch. Then you counted the number of beans required to fill this one cubic inch and multiplied the number by the number of cubic inches in the quart jar. You would be less likely to change this guess, for you know that you have come about as close as possible to the correct number. You will trust your decision.

A sense of values lies at the heart of the weighing of evidence. Fickle judgments are most likely to result from a false or unreliable sense of values.

In the highest center of the brain is that part which gives us a sense of values. This sense of appreciation was one of the last parts of the brain to develop in the process of evolution and it is one of the first parts to be numbed by such anesthetics as chloroform, ether, or alcohol. That is why judgment suffers so much when one drinks to excess.

To guide in the selection of employees for occupations where sound judgment is absolutely essential, psychologists have made up a long list of questions with multiple answers suggested. The candidate taking the test is asked to select the most appropriate answer, indicating his selection by a check mark.

One may have an exceptionally well-developed sense of values in a special field, while his sense of values in other fields, or in life in general, may be rather poor. For example, an artist might possess poor judgment in general but might have exceptionally good judgment where painting or art is concerned. Hence, it is customary to prepare lists of questions that involve a sense of values essential for a certain class of judgment.

In selecting candidates for cadets, the Air Forces have great success with such a list, which is used for determining the likelihood of the cadet developing the type of good judgment that is so essential to safety in flying. A few questions of a similar nature are given below. The applicant is asked to examine the group of answers suggested for each question or situation in this list, and to place a check mark opposite the correct or most logical assumption. The test determines the candidate's sense of values in this field.

1. The most desirable quality a pilot may possess is:

(a) Intelligence.

(b) Skill.

(c) Judgment.

(d) Good health.

(e) Confidence.

2. Precision is essential in military flying because:

(a) Each pilot is a cog in a machine.

(b) Airplanes so often fly close to each other in formation.

(c) All military operations must be precise.

(d) Precision habits allow the pilot to have his mind free from routine details for more complex problems.

(e) The precision pilot can maneuver within narrower limits.

3. A simulated landing is:

(a) A good landing.

(b) A bad landing.

(c) A landing that is not completed.

(d) A training maneuver.

(e) A test for pilot proficiency.

4. Bombers fly in formation because:

(a) There is safety in numbers.

(b) It makes good military appearance.

(c) They can cover the unprotected points of each other.

(d) Enemy fighters are reluctant to attack a formation.

(e) Formations make mass bombing possible.

5. A pilot is flying cross-country when his oil pressure suddenly drops. He should first:

(a) Call the nearest radio range station and inform them of the nature of his difficulty.

(b) Determine the cause for the loss of oil pressure.

(c) Bail out.

(d) Select a level area in the terrain below him and try to land on it.

(e) Immediately stop the motor to avoid further damage.

6. One leg of a B-17 landing gear cannot be extended because of damages to the extending mechanism (pinion sheared off) . The pilots should:

(a) Land on one wheel, and, until the plane slows sufficiently to prevent serious damage, the wing with the damaged gear should be held off the ground by use of the aileron alone.

(b) Same as above except that both aileron and rudder should be used to hold the wing off the ground.

(c) Fly out over open country, unbolt the ball turret that hangs suspended below the belly and allow it to drop, thus making it possible to retract the operative leg of the landing gear and make a belly landing.

(d) Call the control tower and ask them to contact engineering for instructions.

(e) Retract the operative leg of the landing gear and land without first dropping the ball turret.

In each group there are several answers that are obviously wrong and at least two that require careful consideration. The answers that the candidate makes to these questions provide a clue as to the soundness of his sense of values. Since a good sense of values is the foundation upon which sound judgment is built, these questions also provide a means for determining in advance the degree of judgment that the candidate is likely to develop.

We may inherit a brain that has a capacity for developing a good sense of values, but we are more likely to develop such a sense of values if our parents have a good sense of values, since a child through imitation tends to attach the same values to things as do its parents. In some cases, the child may come to recognize that the parents have a very poor sense of values, possibly through his contacts in school and social activities.

Once he realizes this, he may compensate and still develop an exceptionally fine sense of values.

When a student begins flying, he immediately begins to develop a sense of values for those factors involved in flying. If his instructor possesses a poor sense of values, the student may acquire this same poor sense of values. Of course, the student may recognize that his instructor has a poor sense of values and may compensate, thus developing a good sense of values himself, though this is less likely.

Oscar was proud of his Gull Wing Stinson. He would rather you kicked his wife where no gentleman would ever kick a lady than leave your fingerprints on his plane's glossy cowling.

He was making a cross-country flight with a couple of insurance salesmen as passengers. He landed in a rather short field. The take-off would have to be made down-wind, since there was a mountain at the other approach to the airport. To make matters even worse, the field was rough.

Oscar realized the seriousness of the situation. He refilled his tanks for the return trip with some specially high octane gasoline, then felt better. His two passengers returned with their spirits considerably reinforced by a couple of quarts of Four Roses.

The high octane failed to get him over the fence. He ploughed through it, bending the propeller into a hairpin curve and reducing the motor cowling to the appearance of a tin can with which a couple of boys had been playing shinny.

One of the drunks leaned forward, tapped Oscar on the shoulder, and shouted, "We'll give you two more tries. Then if you don't make it, we're getting out."

Oscar had not weighed the evidence properly. He had used a poor sense of values when he decided that a minor item like high octane gasoline would counteract such weighty items as a down-wind take-off on a short and rough field.

Making the Decision

Your own personal background enters into making the

decision. A judge may ask another judge to preside when he feels that his personal experience in the matter may prejudice his decision. If pilots used equal care in not allowing their personal likes and dislikes to influence their decisions, fewer faulty decisions would be made.

I never knew a better instrument pilot than the Major. And how he enjoyed flying on instruments. If he was going to Dallas, Texas, and the route via El Paso was CAVU all the way, while the route via Albuquerque would take him through a wicked cold front with icing conditions and low ceilings, you may be sure that he would choose to go via Albuquerque.

One murky winter day he took off from Romulus Field, at Detroit, en route to Birmingham, Alabama. The ceiling was 500 feet or less all the way, with light snow and sleet. He had no alternate airport available at which he could make a contact let-down.

Operations and Weather both tried to dissuade him from making the flight, but he had a green instrument card and wore the wings of a Command Pilot, which gave him the authority to sign his own clearance.

He was flying a B-24, and his estimated time of arrival at Birmingham showed that he planned to make the flight in two hours and forty-one minutes. He didn't arrive at Birmingham at the time indicated by his E.T.A. An hour passed and still he did not arrive. No word had been heard from him after he had disappeared into the dark, low-hanging clouds over Romulus. Then, six hours and forty-one minutes after his take-off from Romulus, he crashed into a Tennessee mountain top, near Chattanooga.

He had allowed his love for bad weather and instrument flying to warp his judgment. He was rationalizing: "It can't happen to me—I don't make mistakes." But he made a mistake and it did happen to him.

Sticking to the Decision

One of the oldest rules of flying is that after picking a field for a forced landing one should stick to his original decision, even though he later decides that another field is more attractive.

In such circumstances, here is the advantage of sticking to the original decision: With the decision made, the pilot can give his full attention to getting into the field.

Now, consider the disadvantages encountered in making a change:

1. The pilot's attention is distracted from the problem of getting into the field of his choice by his continually looking over other fields.

2. When he chooses another field at the last minute he has less time to plan a course of action and may find it desirable to make still another choice.

3. In making a second choice he is likely to pick a field that he will be unable to reach or one which he will overshoot.

4. He cannot give the full scrutiny to his second choice that he could give to the original choice and is more likely to overlook some vital factor.

Sometimes new data, such as a ravine in the field of his original choice or a high tension line at its approach, may make a second choice wise. However, such conditions should not have been overlooked in making the original choice. If the airplane was too high for him to see all the details of the terrain, he should first pick the general area in which he intended to land and select the field itself at a lower altitude, where he could see all the details.

It is characteristic of the man who does not stick to his decisions to use little care in making his decisions, since he knows he is quite likely to change his mind anyway. The man who intends to stick to his decisions will use care in making his decisions, since he intends to abide by them.

There is nothing more pitiful than a pilot who cannot trust his own judgment. Yet that is the position in which you may find yourself unless you learn to make your decisions with care and then to stick to them.

As in all things, we must observe some degree of balance

in this matter of sticking to decisions. Many accidents have resulted from a bull-headed determination against reversing a decision. This is best illustrated by the pilot who has never learned to make a 180-degree turn when he runs into bad weather. Even the best of judges are willing to reverse their decisions when new evidence disproves the old.

Judgment enters into every decision we make, whether that decision involves the choice of a necktie or the choice of the casket in which one is to be buried; whether it involves the choice between apologizing to the boss or quitting the job; whether it be a decision to spend a nickel for a bottle of soda pop or to spend millions in developing some new manufacturing process.

Decisions that are continually rehashed, reviewed, and reversed produce a tremendous amount of mental fatigue and consequently detract from our efficiency, in addition to taking our attention away from the important details.

The inability to reach a decision almost always arises from one of the following factors:

1. We may not have all the available data. We may have to gather more data before we can make an intelligent decision.

2. We may not have the data properly organized. We may be compelled to reorganize our data before we can reach a decision.

3. We may not have weighed the evidence impartially— we may have laid our hand on the scale to swing the decision in the direction we wished it to go.

The last factor named is so important that it's worth discussing further.

In the administering of justice in a dictatorship, it has been hinted that, if the dictator wants a man shot, a court might be just a wee bit reluctant to consider any evidence that would tend to show that the defendant might be innocent. Or in our own courts, we may find soft-hearted individuals on the jury who refuse to consider the evidence with impartiality.

A cow belonging to poor old widow Jones strayed onto

the tracks of the New York Central Railroad and was killed. Members of the jury may feel sorry for widow Jones and may wish to see her get far more than the cow is worth. They may also feel that the New York Central, with its millions, will not be greatly injured if it is assessed three times the value of the cow. They may also consider the fact that next time it may be their cow that is killed. They do not consider the evidence impartially. Widow Jones gets a handsome price for her cow.

In similar manner, our own personal desires may cause us to minimize and discriminate against evidence that does not favor the decision that we wish to make. When we are aware that we are not considering the evidence with impartiality, we find it difficult to decide. We realize, either consciously or subconsciously, that we are cheating—that we have our hand on the scales.

Often we are really unaware that we have been impartial in considering the data. Later we may realize that we minimized or discriminated against some of the data because of personal desires. In such cases we are justified in reviewing that decision.

Remember how you used to pluck the petals from a daisy, saying as you plucked each petal in turn—she loves me . . . she loves me not . . . she loves me . . . she loves me not? Sometimes an unconscious desire to avoid responsibility causes us to waver back and forth, in similar fashion, between two choices of action. Regardless of how long we waver, we will never have confidence in a decision reached in this manner.

# 11

# How a Pilot Can Control His Emotions

When we speak of controlling our emotions we are speaking of our sympathetic emotions, not the parasympathetic kind. Let us make clear, once and for all, the difference between the two kinds of emotion.

Sympathetic emotions cause your heart to beat faster. They are the emotions that impel you to action. They are the unpleasant emotions, though sometimes the entire emotional cycle may be so pleasing that you may not regard the emotion that initiated it as unpleasant. Even mild fear or anger may have a pleasant, stimulating effect. We think of fear, anger, rage, and pain when we think of the sympathetic emotions, but there are many others, such as, curiosity and the will-to-win. The sympathetic emotions are exciting.

The parasympathetic emotions are the all-clear signal that action is over and include such emotions as contentment, satisfaction, and resignation. These are the passive emotions that cause you to relax.

Let's suppose it is a mild, balmy evening. You are parked in front of your sweetheart's house, with your arms around her. You don't want a change of any kind. Perhaps you are, even now, sighing and whispering in her ear, "Oh, if this moment could but last forever." Yes, indeed, you would like that, wouldn't you? Everything is just perfect. You are under the spell of your passive or parasympathetic emotions, with no incentive to action.

But there is a change in spite of your wishes. Suddenly, like a thundering wraith, the father of your sweetheart, clad in a nightshirt, a menacing shotgun in his hands, emerges from the house.

He shouts, "I've told you a thousand times to stay away from my daughter!"

Now I will freely grant that there is nothing very "sympathetic" about the appearance of the old man in this belligerent attitude. But his appearance has aroused in you a lot of unpleasant emotions, called sympathetic emotions because they will cause nerve impulses to travel out over the entire sympathetic nervous system, assembling your resources —your energy, power, and strength—for action.

These emotions grow in intensity until action takes place. They make you alert and cause you to think faster. They counteract the feeling of fatigue. They enable you to deliver a powerful punch right at the time it is needed. You couldn't live very effectively without them.

Unless you take some intelligent action, these emotions may grow to the point where the cerebral cortex can no longer inhibit the characteristic reflex activities which are initiated by such emotions. This isn't good, because man has strayed so far from his biological moorings that more often than not such primitive activity defeats intelligent action. It is not in keeping with the circumstances.

Of course, men can develop the ability to inhibit such reflex activity to such an extent that they may be scared yet exhibit few of the common signs of fear. Such ability is often useful, but it is not the correct answer to the problem.

In the first place, the emotion may not be a true portrayal of the conditions facing you. We can think of the sympathetic emotions as emergency warning devices, similar to a burglar alarm or the thermostat of an automatic fire sprinkler, and, like such devices, they are inclined to be oversensitive.

In the absence of all the data, we favor the emotional reaction. Just a hint of danger may cause the emotion of fear to be aroused, when additional data may show that there was no cause for alarm.

For example, a young girl is walking along the edge of the sea-wall, as the gray shadows of dusk are settling over the waterfront. Suddenly, a strong, masculine voice growls, "Make just one move, you little vixen, and into the ocean you go."

The girl's heart stops beating and then hammers furiously. The hair stands straight up on her neck. She gasps, momentarily unable to scream. Then, turning around, she sees that the voice came from a pleasant-looking young sailor who is admonishing the cat he is carrying to lie still.

The girl is soon smiling and stroking the cat's beautiful, furry coat. That's how knowledge and the ability to make quick associations help in dissipating uncalled-for emotions and in keeping other emotions reduced to proportions consistent with the emergency.

Suppose, however, a real need for action arises? Then the sooner you take action, the sooner the emotion will subside. The emotion marshals your energy and strength for action, and until action takes place the emotional tension will grow.

You will observe that men who are reliant and know what to do in an emergency are so busy acting that they display few of the reflex signs of fear, and that such men, when meeting opposition, do not manifest many of the reflex signs of anger.

The emotions muster our resources and strength for action, and the intellect plans and directs the action.

Of course, action may be prevented by frustration. If you were bound hand and foot, either by ropes or by circumstances, you could not act and the emotion would grow. Or you may be frustrated by two conflicting motivations. Thus, the desire to enter into romantic relations with the wife of your neighbor would conflict with the desire to be accepted as one of a group, since the society in which we live does not approve nor accept those who act upon sexual desires as freely as the common animals of the barnyard.

Again, your ability to resolve the conflict will relieve the emotion by making it possible for you to take action.

Since emotion seems destined to grow until it reaches such strength that it will evoke response, what will happen if no action is taken?

1.  We will feel distressed by the emotion, since it is essentially unpleasant, designed to prod us to action.

2.  It will soon grow to such a strength that we will not be able to inhibit the reflex activities which are characteristic of the emotion involved; we will show the characteristic physical signs of fear, anger, or rage.

3.  The emotion has set the heart beating faster, raised the blood pressure, and slowed or stopped the digestive processes. This just can't go on forever without causing damage to the body.

Fortunately, we have mental devices which act as lightning rods to relieve this emotional tension and save the body from injury. These devices are known either as defense mechanisms, because they defend the body from injury, or as escape mechanisms, because they enable the high emotional tension to escape.

These devices work as follows: Since we are unable to take action because of frustration or conflict, the cerebral cortex begins making some absurd associations that cannot lead to intelligent action but do lead to an imaginary mental settlement of the problem. The emotion is relieved by this mental settlement much as it would have been relieved by action.

Sometimes when an individual uses these escape mechanisms continually, particularly when he specializes on one mechanism or device to the exclusion of the others, he fools himself so completely that he is totally unaware that he is using such a device.

These mechanisms serve a useful purpose in acting as a buffer to cushion the shocks of some of the rough spots in life, and they do protect the body from the destructive force of too high an emotional tension.

The harm lies in specializing in the use of one device, or in using it too much. Since it relieves the unpleasantness of emotional tension, there is the danger that we will become so addicted to its use that we will use it to escape action. Instead of taking action we will be content with an imaginary solution to our problems.

When we continually use this sort of mechanism, we suffer the following handicaps:

1. We weaken ourselves by demobilizing the resources and strength which the emotion marshals for action, thus making our action weak and ineffectual.

2. Since, in using such mechanisms, we do not make associations that are consistent with reality, this inconsistency creeps into our thinking so that we do not think logically, and consequently do not act logically. We do not respond intelligently to the stimuli of our environment.

3. The use of such devices may progressively increase to the point where we are considered mentally ill.

Before we study a few of these mechanisms let us make sure that we understand what an escape or defense mechanism is:

1. Some motivation, or drive, is involved in any sympathetic emotion. Perhaps many motivations and drives may be involved in one emotion. The emotion is an automatic device of the nervous system for mobilizing all of our strength, energy, and power—both mental and physical—for action with which to carry out the motivation.

2. Normally, the emotion will grow in strength until it becomes so powerful that some response is evoked.

3. The cerebral cortex, the highest center of the nervous system, can make absurd associations by means of which the problem is solved in our imagination. These mental devices are known as escape or defense mechanisms. They serve as lightning rods to relieve high emotional tension, when action is prevented by frustration or conflict.

4. The individual of strong motivations is the most likely to act effectively and to succeed.

5. If the individual dulls his motivations, if he drains off this emotional tension when it is needed to assemble his resources for action, he diminishes his likelihood of success.

Now we will examine a few of these mechanisms:

1. Johnny Jones is having difficulty in learning to fly. He never even learned to do a good job of flying straight and level. His turns were sloppy. Now that he's working on landings and take-offs, his difficulties seem insurmountable.

One day when Johnny arrives at the airport he finds an aura of excitement enveloping the place. There is an epidemic of some kind, in a far-away town. Thousands of lives can be saved if a few bottles of serum, which have been brought to the airport from a near-by laboratory, can be flown to this distant city.

Every pilot at the airport, however, is laid up with the flu. No one but Johnny can deliver the life-saving serum, and Johnny has never soloed.

Undaunted, Johnny volunteers for the job. He climbs into the plane, makes a graceful take-off—for the first time—and is on his way. He flies through several storms, over unfamiliar terrain, and lands in a tiny cow pasture.

That landing was something to be proud of. His return trip is equally sensational, and he arrives home on one of those stormy days when even the birds are walking. He makes a nice, smooth landing and taxis up to receive the praise of the great crowd which has gathered at the airport to welcome him.

Yes—you've guessed it. Johnny has been doing a little daydreaming, when he should have been giving his full attention to the problem at hand. He has been defeating himself in two ways. He has been dulling his motivation by satisfying it in his imagination, and at the same time he has diverted his attention from solving the problem of actual flying to this fantasy.

This mechanism is often known as the flight into fantasy. Johnny gets his satisfaction from imagining that his motivation is satisfied, leaving little incentive to fulfill it through action. It is so much easier to imagine than to work for fulfillment.

How much faster Johnny would progress if he would give up these absurd daydreams and allow his motivation to drive him to study his problems, to determine exactly what was thwarting him, and then to drill on these points until he has mastered them.

Daydreams can cushion some of the hard, rocky points of life for us, but how they cut down our motivation! A motivation may be so powerful that it distresses us, but by directing it to constructive effort to solve our problems we can jet-propel ourselves to success through the power it gives us.

Suppose we look at the daydream as a powerful sedative. Perhaps it may be legitimate to avail yourself of the use of this sedative when relaxing before a cheery fire, or while lying in your warm, comfortable bed. But no one but a fool would use a sedative when there were things he should do, action to be taken, and work to be accomplished.

2. Poor Midge! He could never make a decent landing or a properly coordinated turn. Midge, however, was daring. On the day he soloed, the other students gathered in the hangar doorway to watch him land.

Midge knew they were watching him and he knew that his landing would be quite likely to reward their yen for amused excitement. He decided to give them something else to talk about. After all, he had more daring and nerve than they had— he'd show them. They would forget all about his bad landing when they told the story of his solo flight.

He flew directly over the center of the airport where all could see his show. He nosed down until the motor was roaring and cowling vibrating, then he pulled up into a sharp, tight loop, at five hundred feet. The trainer stalled on top of the loop, slid off into a spin, and crashed. Midge won't fly again.

This was compensation, or perhaps overcompensation. Midge tried to compensate for his poor flying ability by putting on a daring show. He knew that daring was his strong point and attempted to use it to compensate for his poor ability to land the airplane.

When compensating, the individual selects activities at which he can succeed to counterbalance failure in some field where he lacks skill and ability. When overdone, it is an unbalance that is called overcompensation.

Oftentimes compensation serves one well. An individual who is seriously handicapped physically often makes a great success through compensation. A pilot who lacks depth perception may develop an uncanny ability to judge distances by using perspective.

We should be careful to select worthy activities when we compensate, and should use equal care that we do not over-compensate.

How different it might have been in Midge's case if he had developed an ability to recover gracefully from his bad landings and learned to take advantage of each feature of wind and terrain to compensate for his inability to make smooth landings.

I knew a seventy-year-old paint manufacturer whose visual acuity in both eyes was 20-200. It seemed extremely unwise for him to take up flying. However, he somehow managed to learn to fly, and he flew a number of years. So far as I know, he has not met with a serious accident.

It was a fascinating sight to watch him land. Whenever he came in for a landing, all hands on the airport would be seen dashing out of the lunchroom or running to the hangar doorway to watch it. His vision was not sufficiently acute to enable him to level off properly for a landing. He could see just enough to tell when he was within thirty or forty feet of the ground. He would then break his glide slightly, seldom accomplishing a final leveling off, striking the ground at a slight angle and bouncing into the air. Then he would proceed to make a masterly recovery from the bounce, and taxi nonchalantly up to the hangar.

3. Oscar had a terrific yen for the girls, but they didn't care for Oscar. He was homely, a poor student, and had no flair for either athletics or social activities. Furthermore, I doubt if society would have approved had Oscar fully gratified his sexual desires.

Oscar took up flying and became one of the most capable

pilots I have ever known. He sublimated his sexual drive for something that he could do that was socially acceptable.

Sublimation is one of the escape mechanisms that is favorably regarded if not carried to such outrageous extremes that one becomes a fanatic.

4. George began learning to fly with one of the better flying schools—my own. He progressed normally but was dissatisfied, and I was asked to return his tuition. He went to another school a thousand miles away. He wasn't satisfied there either. He wandered from school to school and the last I heard of him he had spent enough money to have bought a light airplane, and he hadn't even soloed.

George was using the mechanism known as nomadism to get away from conflict. The nomad wanders from spot to spot, even when there is no economic or other advantage to be gained. He is unlikely to succeed because he pulls up stakes and moves when the going gets rough, instead of buckling down and solving his problem.

This nomadism should not be confused with a recognition of the inevitable, wherein, by a process of logical reasoning, one surrenders to the inevitable and withdraws from the field when he realizes that success is impossible. The nomad rationalizes that there is no use bucking your head against a stone wall when the green pastures beyond the horizon have no stone walls. He gives up and moves to what he hopes will be a happier hunting ground, when all that was needed was a little perseverance and diligent effort. The nomad becomes a quitter, justifying his action by saying that he is moving to greener pastures.

5. Lucy was a vivacious little butterfly who decided to add flying to her many accomplishments. She selected my flying school. Like all students, she had her difficulties.

It wasn't long before I noticed that she was climbing wearily out of her long, chromium-plated convertible, clutching her hand to her head with the expression of a suffering Madonna. Then she began complaining that she had a splitting headache at the end of each flight. A time came when she would beg me to take her in before a lesson was completed. "I can't stand this awful headache," she would wail.

One day when I had taxied back to the hangar less than ten minutes after take-off, I said, "Just a minute, Miss Lucy, let's do something for that headache."

I sent one of the other students to the hangar office for a box of aspirin tablets and a glass of water. By the time she had taken three of the tablets and washed them down with a glass of water, the other students had gathered around the airplane and were taking in every word.

I said, "Miss Lucy, you show more promise than any student I have ever trained." I must confess that I had my fingers crossed, but drastic measures were needed and I was gratified by the pleased interest that appeared on her face.

I continued, "It is too bad that these headaches have to interfere with your phenomenal progress just when you are doing so good. If aspirins will just stop your headaches so that we won't have to interrupt your lessons, we will soon have an aviatrix on this field who can really fly an airplane."

Lucy's headaches disappeared as if by magic and she never complained of another as long as I knew her.

I have no doubt that Lucy had really been suffering from headaches which were very real to her. She was using the mechanism known as hysteria. When one meets a difficult problem, he may unconsciously wish that he was sick so that he might dodge it or put it off until some more advantageous moment. Then, obligingly enough, the mental devices provide the imaginary headache that is so real to the victim. Of course, it may be almost any ailment. This condition commonly goes by the name of psychoneurosis.

6. Tony designed and built an airplane that was a whiz. It was fast. It was smooth and responded so nicely to the controls that pilots described the control action as being like velvet. It seemed to have just everything, and Tony was very proud of it.

The C.A.A. engineering inspector agreed with Tony that the plane was a good performer. He agreed that all the praise it was receiving was justified. "There's just one thing," he said. "There is a little aileron flutter in a dive and I think you will have to change the design of the rear spar, lest it fail in a dive."

"I'll show you how much *-!!!!**- chance there is of its failing in a dive!" shouted Tony in anger. Before anyone could stop him, he had jumped into the airplane and was climbing high into the sky. In his anger he had not taken the precaution of donning a parachute.

Down he came in a screaming dive. There was a loud crackling sound, followed by a muffled, shattering report, as the airplane disintegrated in mid-air. Tony was killed.

That airplane was Tony's big dream fulfilled. He had noticed the flutter but didn't think it was serious. He had tried to eliminate it but couldn't, and he felt frustrated when the inspector called his attention to it. He projected his feeling into the airplane and took it out in a punishing dive that the airplane could not withstand.

Students often project their own faults to the person of their instructor. He doesn't know how to teach, or he is deliberately holding them back to get more money out of them.

Perhaps this is as good a time as any to discuss the much-touted inferiority complex. Desires and wishes that are in direct conflict with the approved aims or the accepted goal of the individual are unpleasant and troublesome. The satisfaction of such desires results in a feeling of guilt or inferiority. This is the basis of the inferiority complex.

Thus, engaging in erotic practices that would be in direct conflict with one's aims in life and with his ideals might well be expected to produce a feeling of guilt or an inferiority complex. Sometimes one represses the very thought of the sexual desires, but the needs are there, causing a feeling of guilt. From such repressions spring such changes to personality as are evidenced in the prudish old maid. Of course, inferiority complexes spring from many sources other than sex.

It seems to be a good idea to keep these things that give us a feeling of guilt out in the open, evaluating them by intelligent reasoning. One may recognize the sex drive with no feeling of guilt, awaiting fulfillment in the future, when he is married and when such fulfillment will not be contrary to social acceptance. In such a manner, sex can grow into something beautiful to which one can look forward.

We will enumerate a few of those things that so often cause a flying student to develop an inferiority complex:

A. A bright student may discover that his ability to develop new reflexes and to develop co-ordination does not compare favorably with that of other students. This will mean that he will have to work harder and put in more hours of practice to qualify, and he is unwilling to admit this necessity, though he does unconsciously realize it.

He should realize that there is nothing to feel guilty about in such a situation. Most intellectuals learn skills slowly because their intellects exert a strong inhibitory influence over the reflexes and insist on controlling each detail instead of letting the automatic reflex action take over. His instructor may be hinting at just this condition when he says, "You try too hard. Relax and take it easy."

If the student is going to learn to fly, he must apply himself and practice. This will have to be done, no matter how much he may rebel against it. He is wise to accept reality and cheerfully go to work.

B. He may become envious and even jealous of other students who learn with greater ease and seem more proficient. Here again, he should realize that, if he applies himself diligently, he too can become a proficient pilot. He should refuse to compare his progress with that of other students. His own progress is all that counts, and any relation between it and the progress of other students is unimportant.

C. He may have some physical disability that did not show up on his physical or a defect for which he has a waiver. Or he may have some trait of temperament that he imagines may handicap him in flying.

He should get these things into the open and evaluate

them, take his instructor into his confidence and tell him about his problem. Nine times out of ten, his instructor knows that his particular defect doesn't mean a thing and will tell him so. If he is handicapped, there is no point in dodging the issue, for his instructor is in a better position to help him to overcome the handicap once the instructor is made aware of it.

7. To return to the escape mechanisms: We are now ready to tackle the king-pin of them all, so far as the airplane pilot is concerned—rationalizing.

When one rationalizes, he ascribes false motives to his behavior in an attempt to bolster his ego. The case of the fox and the wild grapes is a classic example. Pollyanna was a gay, little rationalizer. There are many occasions in life when rationalizing may soften the way, but flying is not one of those occasions.

Here are some of the dangerous forms that rationalizing may take:

(a)    "It can't happen to me," and, "I never make any serious mistakes."

I have never liked the word "overconfident," because I believe that one cannot possess too much confidence. But one can possess false confidence. "It can't happen to me," and "I never make any serious mistakes," are often responsible for false confidence—false because the individual is not basing the belief that he can succeed on past performance, but upon a feeling that he is lucky, that somehow fate will take care of him. "It can happen to others but not to me. Others make mistakes, but not me."

(b)  "Fate is against me." "The sun was in my eyes," etc.

Here again, the individual is placing the responsibility upon fate, thus excusing himself. This type of rationalizing breeds a lack of confidence and can greatly undermine the pilot's flying ability.

In both cases the individual is making an excuse for his actions that is not consistent with reality.

Possibly the most dangerous form, so far as the pilot is

concerned, is, "It can't happen to me," and, "I never make any serious mistakes."

The motor quit, just beyond the boundaries of the airport, as Jimmy was taking off. Jimmy knew that one should not attempt to turn back; that pilots had been killed attempting to do so. But Jimmy also felt, "It can't happen to me." He did. It did. And they buried Jimmy.

Johnny knew that pilots have been killed buzzing the houses of their girl friends. But he felt, "It can't happen to me." That's why Johnny isn't flying today.

Fifty miles out of Washington, with rough country ahead, Charlie should have checked his fuel supply to be sure. Nevertheless he felt, "I never make any serious errors, and I measured my fuel before I started on this trip. I couldn't be wrong—no need to check again." But Charlie was wrong and he crashed in rough, wooded country.

A physiological drive, such as the desire to seek oxygen, can be frustrated just so long and then something must happen. Since our motivations are built upon our physiological drives, much the same thing applies to the frustration of our motivations. Individuals have various degrees of tolerance for frustration. Some people can hold their breath much longer than others, thus frustrating the drive to seek oxygen. When this tolerance for frustration is exceeded, the escape devices save the organism from injury.

Unfortunately, we often use these escape devices to escape action when we are frustrated only by our own inertia or, to put it more bluntly, by our own damn laziness, either mental or physical. At other times, our frustration would be avoided if we possessed more knowledge or training. Many conflicts yield to a solution when we correctly evaluate them and use intelligent logical reasoning.

Action relieves emotion. Knowledge and confidence make quick, decisive action possible. One who possesses these qualities is not likely to succumb to emotion or to seek relief from emotion through the use of escape devices.

Emotion rises to the danger point when you are faced with a situation that you are unable to solve. You may be unable to solve the problem because you are frustrated by physical barriers; perhaps you lack the mental capacity, the physical capacity, or both the mental and physical capacity necessary to solve the problem. In such a case, emotion, through marshaling your resources, may make it possible for you to solve the problem.

Often your difficulty may be a conflict between two motivations. In such a case, it is necessary to decide which motivation you will act upon before effective action can be taken.

We will consider a simple case of conflict between two motivations: You should spend the night studying to prepare yourself for an examination. That is one motivation. You want to take Mary Jane to a preview of a new picture. That is another motivation and it conflicts with the first motivation, since you cannot do both.

Suppose you are unable to resolve the conflict. You get nowhere studying for the examination because you are trying to make up your mind whether or not to take Mary Jane to the preview. You keep Mary Jane on tenterhooks because you cannot decide. She will be angrier than if you had told her you had to study and could not take her. Consequently, your action is ineffective all around.

We will consider three general sources of conflict, bearing in mind that there may be overlapping, that is, a conflict may spring from two or even all three of the sources.

1. Conflict between a direct action that has little chance for success, and an indirect action that is more certain to succeed; the conflict between having satisfaction right now or foregoing immediate satisfaction for the sake of a more certain chance of fulfillment.

Knowing that the higher specialized motivation offers greater possibility for fulfillment, we are still tempted to act upon the lower motivation because it seems to promise quicker results. Hence, we have a conflict as to whether we shall try for quick results or forego immediate satisfaction for the sake of more certain fulfillment.

2.    Conflict between a primitive motivation and the motivation that causes us to wish to be accepted by the group.

In his primitive state, man often had to hide from or flee from danger. He often had to fight and destroy his enemies. Like the wild animal, he was compelled to do these things in order that he might survive. But man has built a better way of life for himself in which he and his fellows live in greater safety and are provided with a greater abundance of the good things of life through learning, building, and creating, rather than through destroying; through co-operating, rather than through fighting each other.

In many situations those who hide or flee from danger, or who fight and destroy their enemies, are not accepted by the group because of such behavior. Hence, a conflict arises between the desire to yield to a primitive motivation and the desire to be accepted by the group.

3.    Conflict between a lower motivation and the motivation that causes us to desire to be accepted by our God.

Even though a primitive motivation may be acceptable to the group, the individual may not believe that it will be acceptable to his God. Hence, a conflict exists between the desire to act upon the primitive motivation and the desire to be accepted by God.

With no implication as to moral values, we will speak of the motivations closer to our physiological drives as our lower motivations, and the motivations that are farther removed from our physiological drives as our higher motivations.

The greater a capacity one has to learn, the more motivations he will develop. Hence, the intelligent person is likely to have more motivations, more likelihood of conflict, than does the less intelligent person. But the more intelligent person may learn to resolve his conflicts quickly, and that is the important difference.

A man who always acted upon primitive motivations might act with great effectiveness because of a lack of conflict. Such an individual would quite likely be a Dillinger, a Clyde Barrow, or a Pretty Boy Floyd.

We are forced to make a choice. The quicker we make that choice, the more effective our action will be. Where the conflict has been quickly settled, we are likely to have our emotions under control.

However, it is important that we make the proper choice, for if we make a choice that we do not believe is right, we may suffer from a feeling of guilt and thereby lose some of our effectiveness. The college student who should be studying for the exam might decide to take Mary Jane to the preview instead and might feel guilty and depressed throughout the evening. He might even act in a boorish manner toward Mary Jane as a result, thus defeating his objective.

Man has risen to his present high estate through learning new motivations. The penalty of so many motivations is conflict, since to act upon one motivation often means acting contrary to the fulfillment of another motivation. The solution lies in developing the ability to resolve these conflicts quickly.

In nearly all of the situations that arise in our civilized life, we will be wise to choose the motivations that drive us to learn, to build, to create, and to co-operate, rather than the motivations that drive us to destroy and to fight our fellows.

If we choose constructive motivations to act upon, the succeeding motivations that we build are likely to be a specialized means of fulfilling those constructive motivations.

If we choose motivations that drive us to destroy and to fight our fellowman, the motivations built upon such destructive motivations are likely to be a specialized means of destroying and fighting.

Adolph Hitler apparently sought to attain his ends by fighting and by destroying, and some of his more highly specialized motivations were more fiendish than his primitive emotions.

With so many motivations built up from our physiological drives, we often find such conflict between two motivations that to act upon one motivation opposes acting upon another. In such a case, the emotion tends to force action. We are forced to resolve the conflict or it may resolve itself, either through some mental device, a purely imaginary solution, or through forcing reflex responses that are characteristic of that particular emotion.

When we fail to act, because of either frustration or conflict, the emotion grows to the point where reflex responses that characterize the particular emotion take place without any voluntary desire for such responses on our part. It is through these reflex responses that other people recognize that we are subjected to the emotion.

To a great degree, we can train ourselves to inhibit these reflex responses. This is often beneficial, but it is even better to learn to resolve our conflicts, to be prepared, and to act.

# 12
# The Mood to Win

"Ummm! Isn't she gorgeous? Well proportioned, nicely streamlined, and no doubt a sweet flying job. But maybe a bit too fast and tricky for me."

You mask such flighty, amorous thoughts behind a smug air of indifference as you seat yourself on a stool beside her at the soda fountain.

You are much too polite to stare directly at her but you slyly run your eyes over her reflected image in the fountain mirror, giving that image your full approval.

She is nicely cowled-in, with the exception of certain parts so well streamlined by nature that there is obviously no possibility of improvement.

Your eyes rove upward, noting the inviting curves of a well-formed mouth, with a pert little nose mounted above it at a jaunty angle. Then you notice the large, blue eyes, fringed with long, dark lashes.

Those eyes undergo some sudden metamorphosis. You look hastily aside and your face reddens as you suddenly discover that those eyes are staring directly into your own, flashing annoyance mingled with resentment.

I am in the front seat of my Swallow training plane, and the eyes staring back at me from the little mirror attached to the strut before me are the eyes of my student, a salesman named Hutchins. I often see a mistake coming, in the emotions reflected from this little mirror. I suspect that Hutch studies me as much as I study him. Right now he is probably wondering what my next move will be.

Something is wrong with Hutch today. This isn't the first time he has done such a lousy job of flying. One day he does a superb job of flying, with all the smooth confidence of the "natural" flier; then the next time I have him up for a lesson he makes every mistake in the book with an exasperating clumsiness that marks him as my number one problem student.

I see E. B. Slaw, a competitor who is attempting to start a rival school adjacent to mine, peering out at us from the doorway of his hangar as we taxi in at the completion of the lesson.

Hutch's landing resembles the flying-farmer-act at an air circus. I realize that Slaw must be speculating on the possibility of enticing Hutch over to his school.

Hutch is buying flying time by the hour and can make a change any time he wants to. From the look in his eyes, I have a hunch that he is ripe to make a change if I don't pull a rabbit out of a hat right quickly.

Slaw is walking over to join us. Before he gets within earshot, I turn quickly to Hutch and ask, "How would you like to save half the money you are spending on flying lessons?"

Hutch replies cynically, "Maybe it would be better if I saved all the money I'm spending on my flying."

Making no comment to this biting rejoinder, I call to a mechanic to roll the airplane into the hangar and, taking Hutch by the arm, I hurry him over to my battered old Ford before Slaw can join us.

"Where are we going?" Hutch asks, as we roll out onto the highway.

"I want you to meet a friend of mine who makes his living playing the ponies," I reply. "When this friend of mine is not out at the race track, he hangs out in this little tavern, a mile up the road from the airport. I want you to listen in on something he can tell us about horses. Last night he told me something about horses that may also apply to pilots."

We are in luck. My friend Scotty is seated alone at his favorite booth in the tavern. As soon as the introductions are over and I have ordered beers for Scotty and Hutch, and a jcoke for myself, I say to Scotty, "My friend Hutch is interested in your method for picking the winners. I wish you'd tell it to him

160

just as you told it to me last night."

Scotty's face lights up with enthusiasm. "Glad to," he replies. "But see here," he warns Hutch, "you let me pick 'em for you. You gotta spend a lifetime around the stables, figuring dopesheets and studying horses before you can do yourself any good picking 'em."

He sets his beer mug down on the table and wipes the froth from his lips with the back of his hand. "You see, I know the running time of all the nags and I am always studying the dopesheets. I pick the winner scientifically, but that ain't enough. Before I lay any dough on the line, I go down and look at my horse. If he is nervous, fidgety, or snaps at me, I'm likely to cancel my bet on him. I simply don't bet on a horse, even if he seems a cinch to win, unless he's in the right mood."

Hutch looks a little surprised and I can see that he is interested.

Scotty hurriedly points out, "They match up the horses for a race so that all the horses in the race have about the same running time. Any one of them could win. That's what makes it a race.

"A horse must put on its very best performance if it is to win, and it just can't put on its best performance unless it is in the right mood."

"You mean a horse just doesn't have any pep on some days?" Hutch questions.

Scotty nods excitedly, hurrying to add, "But that's only part of it. Sometimes a horse is so nervous and jumpy that you know it will most likely get off to a poor start. Then again a horse may want to fight instead of running, and slows down to nip at the other horses."

On the way back to the airport, Hutch says, "I seem to get the idea that you think my moods have something to do with my flying."

It is really a question, and I reply with a question. "What do you think? Look back over the days you have flown. One day you are hot and the next day you're cold. One day you are at your best and the next day you are lousy. Say! Just how do you go about selecting the days you fly?"

For a moment Hutch looks a little startled. Then a happy grin spreads across his face. "Damned if I don't believe you've hit it!"

He rushed on. "I sell radios. My time is my own and I work when I feel like it. When I sell half a dozen radios all in a row, I often decide that I've done enough for the day and knock off work and head out to the airport for a flying lesson.

"Other days, everything just seems to go wrong. I don't sell a single radio. I seem to antagonize my prospects. I decide that I'm killing future sales and that, since I am not getting anywhere, I might as well quit for the day and take a flying lesson."

We hurry back to the airport to examine Hutch's logbook. We check back. Sure enough, on the days when Hutch sold a lot of radios he also did a good job of flying. On days when he failed to sell any radios, he also failed to accomplish much at the controls of an airplane.

Hutch is enthusiastic by this time. "You're right," he says.

"I can save about half the money I spend on flying lessons by staying away from the airport when I'm not in the right mood to fly."

Later Hutch asks me the sixty-four dollar question: "What is mood?" and then, "Wouldn't it be nice if we could slip out of one mood and into another as easy as changing clothes?"

Within reasonable limits we can learn to do that very thing; we can learn to change our moods. Hutchins had no need to change his mood when his confident mood accompanied him to the flying field, but he needed a change when his discouraged mood followed him to the field.

We might compare this lag in our change of mood to a situation wherein troops were moved so hurriedly from an Arctic post that they arrived at a new post in the desert still wearing the same heavy clothing they had been wearing in the Arctic. At this new post such clothing might prove a serious handicap to them, just as Hutchins's discouraged mood proved a handicap to him when flying.

On the other hand, had these Arctic troops been transferred to a post in Northern Minnesota, during the cold winter months, their heavy arctic clothing might have proved as welcome to them as Hutchins's confident mood was to him when flying.

Mood is a word used to describe the relative sensitivity that characterizes our reaction to the various emotional Stimuli.

When an emotion has been aroused, we become increasingly sensitive to the very stimuli that serve to arouse such an emotion. As the emotion grows in strength, our sensitivity to such stimuli also grows.

When action has been blocked, it is as though a dam had been erected to stop our flow of action—like building a dam across a stream. Our emotions build up behind this barrier to action, just as water would build up behind the dam across the stream.

As this emotional pressure or tension mounts, we become increasingly sensitive to the very stimuli that produce the emotions; a mood develops that is dominated by the emotions involved.

Suppose we compare the situation with the manner in which a police force might be alerted from the stimuli of a number of thieves operating in a certain district.

The chief of police looks up from the morning reports. "I see O'Niel's warehouse was broken into last night. Better add another policeman to that warehouse district—apparently one isn't enough."

Suppose there is another robbery the next night. The chief fumes. "Put two more policemen on that warehouse beat tonight. We're going to put a stop to those robberies."

This might continue until there were a dozen policemen patrolling the warehouse district that ordinarily was handled by one man. The district is alerted. The law is in a position to be extremely sensitive to what takes place in the warehouse district

163

and will take vigorous action upon any trifling incident that arouses the slightest suspicion. The chief may see fit to maintain this vigilant patrol of the warehouse district for several weeks after the robberies have ceased.

In like manner, our emotions, when aroused, make us sensitive to, and cause us to react vigorously to, any stimuli that may foster such emotions. We call this state of emotional alertness a mood.

For instance: Any wary bachelor knows that if a girl is in a mood for matrimony he must be exceedingly cautious not to make any remark that might even remotely resemble a proposal of marriage, lest she grab him by the arm and drag him to the nearest parson.

If you are in a scary mood, the creak of a board in a darkened warehouse may cause your heart to start hammering against your ribs and your hair to stand on end. If you are in an angry mood, a bit of friendly banter may cause you to explode with anger. If you are in a discouraged mood, any little difficulty may be magnified to a calamity.

Whereas, if you are in a confident mood, such little difficulties serve only to spur you to act with greater vigor.

Suppose that for the purpose of study we divide our moods into classifications according to the emotions that dominate such moods, making no attempt to compile complete lists but setting down a few characteristic types in each classification.

Our first division will separate the moods dominated by the sympathetic emotions from the moods dominated by the parasympathetic emotions.

Then we will separate the less desirable emotions from the more desirable emotions in each of the foregoing classifications.

THE SYMPATHETIC EMOTIONS

| Less Desirable | More Desirable |
| --- | --- |
| Anger | Elation |

| Fear | Curiosity |
| Rage | The Will-to-Win |
| Jealousy | Wonder |
| Hate | |

## THE PARASYMPATHETIC EMOTIONS

| Less Desirable | More Desirable |
| Despondence | Contentment |
| Resignation | Satisfaction |
| Peace | |

Our sympathetic emotions speed up the activity of the nervous system. The nerve impulses go hurtling along the neurons and across the synapses at greater speed when our mood is dominated by our sympathetic emotions. This speed ordinarily leads to more effective response.

When our mood is dominated by a parasympathetic emotion, the nervous system operates at a slower tempo that is suitable to relaxation and sleep.

It is important to note that the relationship between the speed at which the nervous system operates and the mood that dominates us is an equation that works both ways.

Slow Mental Activity (Fosters & Produces) A mood dominated by parasympathetic

Rapid Mental Activity (Fosters & Produces) A mood dominated by sympathetic

This bit of knowledge makes available to us a host of physical devices that we may find useful in modifying our emotions and our moods, since those factors that speed the activity of the nervous system may prove useful to us in switching from a depressed, lethargic, or relaxed mood to a mood that is more desirable for action, while those factors that slow nervous activity may prove useful to us when we wish to relax. There is nothing baffling or confusing about these tangible factors, and it requires no great amount of practice to learn to use them effectively.

We will compile a list of the factors that tend to speed the activity of the nervous system and another list of the factors that tend to slow the activity of the nervous system.

Factors That Tend to Speed Mental Activity

1. The sympathetic emotions and the moods that are dominated by the sympathetic emotions.

2. A refreshed physical state. Such a state is encouraged by the factors listed below.

(a) Progressive thinking.

(b) Variety of activity.

(c) Recreation.

(d) Sufficient relaxation, rest, and sleep.

3. A wholesome state of health.

4. Pain. (This is an undependable factor since continuous pain, or pain to the extreme, where it produces shock, seems to slow mental activity.)

5. Cold. (Cold stimulates the sympathetic nervous system; cool, fresh air and cold showers may speed mental activity. However, continuous exposure to extreme cold can use so much of the body's energy that the speed of nervous activity will eventually be slowed.)

6. Food. (Several universities have conducted tests wherein one group of students was given light snacks at intervals during a rigorous series of examinations. These students who were given the snacks passed their examinations with higher grades than did the control group that received no snacks.

The nervous system has no means of storing fuel. When the sugar level of the blood falls below a normal point, the activity of the nervous system slows because of an insufficient supply of fuel. However, heavy meals slow the activity of the nervous system, since a stomach full of food requires activity upon the part of the digestive apparatus, a normal activity of the parasympathetic system. Hence, a stomach full of food will act as a stimulus to the parasympathetic emotions.)

7. Sympathomimetic drugs. (The caffeine found in tea, coffee, and many Cola drinks is a mild sympathomimetic drug that acts as a stimulant to the central nervous system, thereby speeding activity. Adrenin, the secretion produced by the medulla of the adrenals, is a powerful sympathomimetic drug.)

Factors That Tend to Slow Mental Activity

1. The parasympathetic emotions and the moods that are dominated by the parasympathetic emotions.

2. Fatigue. (Fatigue is fostered by the factors listed below:

(a) Worrying and other types of dead-end thinking.

(b) Monotony.

(c) Lack of relaxation, rest, and sleep.

(d) Concentration and deep thinking. These, of course, are useful and not to be discouraged, since fatigue arising from such sources may be compared to the physical fatigue that arises from useful physical labor.)

3. The toxins of disease.

4. Sedatives. (Alcohol is a sedative, although it produces a false feeling of stimulation through relieving our inhibitions.)

5. A heavy meal.

6. Lack of oxygen. (This is important to the pilot flying at high altitudes, since his mental activity may be slowed to the point where he will lose consciousness unless he has a supplemental source of oxygen available. Lack of oxygen is treacherous to the pilot, since it often produces a false feeling of stimulation somewhat akin to that produced by alcohol. As a result, a pilot may be unaware that he is operating at a lowered efficiency and he may actually lose consciousness.)

7. An abnormally low level of sugar in the blood.

8. Centrifugal acceleration. (Centrifugal acceleration, as

when a pilot is pulling out of a dive, drains the blood from the brain and forces it into the abdominal area, resulting in a slowing of the activity of the nervous system. If the pull-out is extreme, the pilot may suffer from black-out; that is, a gray-black screen may appear before his eyes, and he may even lose consciousness. As a rule, no serious after-effects, so far as the nervous system is concerned, follow black-out. It is important that the pilot realize that he operates at a lowered efficiency during violent maneuvers, even though he may not actually suffer from black-out.)

9. Centripetal acceleration. (When exposed to centripetal acceleration, as when the pilot is performing inverted maneuvers, the blood is forced into the brain under pressure. Extreme centripetal acceleration may produce red-out, that is, a pinkish red screen may appear before the eyes, and if the acceleration is severe enough the pilot may lose consciousness.)

Extreme centripetal acceleration may cause serious injury to the brain. Tiny blood vessels are often ruptured, and centripetal accelerations of 5 g or 6 g may cause death.

Black-out is not produced at the instant of the pull-out since the effects of the loss of blood from the brain are not instantly apparent. This is fortunate, as it enables the pilot to complete or nearly complete the pull-out before the loss of consciousness.

There is no apparent lag in red-out. The moment the pressure is exerted upon the brain the pilot loses consciousness.

For the purpose of discovering how a change in the speed of mental activity may produce a change in mood, suppose we consider the case of our friend, Jake Lund, who has decided to end his life.

It seems hours that Jake has sat staring vacantly at the rope he is holding in his hands. He is picturing himself standing on the nail-keg, tying that rope around a rafter that spans the driveway in the barn. He rises slowly to his feet, and with his head bowed as though he did not possess the strength to hold it erect, he shuffles toward the barn.

Suddenly two figures leap out of the semi-darkness and seize him. They drag him back into the house.

The mean-looking one, whose face is marred by a livid scar, snarls at Jake, "We're after that money you've been salting away. Show us where you've hidden it."

Jake slowly shakes his head. He mutters, "You fools! I haven't a cent. They're foreclosing the mortgage on my farm tomorrow."

A vicious sneer appears on the face of the mean-looking thief. He slaps Jake, following the slap with a kick in the groin. Jake doubles over in pain.

His tormentor gloats. "That'll show you we mean business. We're going to have that money if we have to kill you to get it."

"Speak up!" says the man who is holding Jake. "He'll roast your toes with hot coals if you don't talk."

The mean one slaps Jake again, then queries a threat. "You going to talk or do we have to get the fire started in the stove?"

Jake suddenly breaks away from the man who is holding him and lunges at his tormentor. During the next few minutes this man who had intended to kill himself is engaged in a furious battle for survival. The battle ends with the two bandits securely bound with. the rope Jake had intended to knot about his own neck.

Jake snapped out of his depressed mood just as you have seen a person snap out of a similar depressed mood, as he leaped and ran to escape from a truck that was roaring down upon him, just after he had exclaimed, "I wish I were dead!" No doubt his professed desire to die was as real to him, as was Jake's determination to end his own life, but the sympathetic emotions, when aroused, speed mental activity to the point where a depressed mood cannot persist.

Had there been a competent physician at hand when Jake determined to end his life, the physician could have shaken Jake out of his depressed mood through the administration of some powerful sympathomimetic drug. The emotions aroused through Jake's encounter with the bandits caused his own glands to produce and secrete into his blood stream a powerful sympathomimetic drug—adrenin—and Jake was jolted out of his depressed mood.

Fatigue produces results opposite to the effects produced by a sympathomimetic drug. Fatigue slows the activity of the nervous system.

The nervous system suffers excess fatigue when one indulges in dead-end thinking and worrying. When a thought or an association repeats itself continually—as it does when one worries or indulges in dead-end thinking—certain pathways in the nervous system are subjected to continuous usage. These pathways are composed of chains of nerve cells. We call these nerve cells neurons, and the junctions between the neurons are known as synapses.

When a neuron is stimulated continuously, the by-products of metabolism accumulate in the area of the synapse. This accumulation of the by-products of metabolism, within the synapse, interferes with the transmission of the nerve impulse across the synapse from one neuron to another, thus slowing and sometimes blocking mental activity.

The synapses, common to pathways that are subjected to fatigue through continuous usage, are also common to other pathways, just as the junctions of a boulevard may also serve the side streets that cross the boulevard. If these intersections on a boulevard were closed, traffic would also be closed on the hundreds of cross streets as well as on the boulevard.

In fact, you have seen this happen when a circus or a ball park is disgorging its traffic onto a single street. Traffic throughout the entire city may be slowed because of the traffic snarl on this one street, since the junctions blocked on this street cause hundreds of other streets to become blocked.

This congestion of traffic is similar to what happens in the nervous system when, through worrying or any other form of dead-end thinking, we use a few pathways continuously, thus slowing mental activity not only on those pathways but throughout the nervous system.

Ordinarily we think progressively. We make an association and it serves as a springboard to a new association, so that we do not use one pathway continuously. At times, we are unable to reach a new association. We have come to a dead-end and keep repeating the old associations over and over in an attempt to reach some new association. This continuous usage of a few pathways produces undue fatigue.

There are occasions, however, when concentration and deep thinking are essential, and the resultant fatigue that is produced may be likened to the physical fatigue that is produced by useful work.

Suppose we consider a few of our more desirable sympathetic emotions: curiosity, the will-to-win, and elation. Curiosity drives us to learn. The will-to-win drives us to complete what we are doing, in an effective manner. Elation drives us to strike while the iron is hot, to deliver the "coup de grace" when we perceive that things are coming our way.

Response to such emotions seldom causes us to clash head-on with our fellows, since such activity is socially acceptable. Moods built upon such emotions make us sensitive to the stimuli that drive us to effective action. Such moods sweep us on toward success.

The less desirable emotions, such as hate, fear, anger, rage, and jealousy, enabled man to survive in his primitive state just as a wild animal survives through hiding or fleeing from danger and through fighting and destroying its enemies. If you and I were to respond to these emotions as fully as do the wild animals, we might become a Dillinger, a Jesse James, or even an Adolf Hitler.

These primitive emotions can lead to effective action of their kind when they are not hampered by emotional conflict, but man has learned to forge a more abundant life for himself through creating and building instead of destroying. Man frowns upon response to these destructive emotions. Those who do act without restraint upon such emotions are not likely to be accepted by the group. The desire to be accepted by the group is a powerful motivation, and it clashes head-on with these violent emotions in many phases of our civilized life. Such a clash produces mental conflict. The emotion grows in strength as a result of this conflict, and our action is often made ineffective.

How Can We Deal Effectively with These Emotions?

1. Sometimes we act upon them.

Even in his civilized state, there may be times when it becomes desirable for man to hide or to flee from danger. There may even be times when it becomes necessary to fight and destroy his enemies. We can learn to recognize such situations and to go promptly into action. When we act, the emotion is less likely to pyramid to great heights.

In those situations where man must act upon these violent emotions in the interests of his own survival, such action seldom arouses the disapproval of his group. There is consequently little likelihood of mental conflict.

2. We can turn from destructive effort to building, creating, and learning.

If we have planned our behavior in advance for such situations, we are more likely to resolve the conflict promptly before the destructive emotion has opportunity to grow and before a mood dominated by such an emotion can develop.

3. Insight can help.

There are situations wherein there is no doubt that we should act upon our primitive emotions, but there are more situations wherein it is clear that we should act constructively, rather than yield to these less desirable emotions.

Between these definitely marked situations, there lies a vast no man's land of borderline cases where we may have some doubt as to how we should act. These borderline cases produce most of our conflicts. Sometimes a sudden insight leads us to understand, and causes us to feel emotionally, that one side of this emotional conflict is so weak that it is utterly ridiculous. We see the incongruity. At this point, humor seems to be nature's transitional device that accompanies the quick change of emotion that occurs. Some automatic mental reflex of which we are not conscious seems to produce this sudden insight.

Through this sudden insight some situation of dignity suddenly loses much of its dignity. Or something that seems omnipotent loses much of its all-powerful aspect, or something that seemed immense or colossal melts to insignificance.

The sudden emotional change produced by this sudden insight is accompanied by the twinkle in the eye, the soft low chuckle, or perhaps, the deep belly-laugh. If we are pleased by this sudden insight, we readily accept it and it seems funny to us, as we recognize the incongruity of the situation. If this sudden insight is not so welcome, we resist accepting it, and hence the emotional change may come slower, if at all, and little or no humor results.

For instance, a pompous, arrogant politician, clothed in great dignity—as well as in his long tails and tall silk hat— steps on a banana peel and, amid wild gyrations, crashes to the sidewalk. All his dignity is gone, and the incongruity of the situation tickles us. We readily accept his loss of dignity because it pleases us to see him embarrassed. But if a child or some sweet old lady steps on a banana peel and falls with a corresponding loss of dignity we do not so readily accept this sudden change. We wish it hadn't happened and it may not seem funny.

In like manner, emotions may build up to an importance so out of keeping with the circumstances that a sudden insight may cause us to see the incongruity. If we are pleased to see such emotions cut down to size, we are amused and laugh. If we cherish and wish to maintain the emotions involved, we are less likely to see any humor in the situation.

As an example, fear may be such an unwelcome emotion that we wish to rid ourselves of it. If some sudden insight reduces this emotion to such diminutive size that it seems incongruous, we readily accept the change and laugh. But if we are angry we may wish to stay angry; we do not wish to be mollified or appeased, and the automatic reflex of the intellect that would bring us this sudden insight fails to function. We see nothing funny about the situation.

Perhaps men who have a keen sense of humor and are always ready to laugh at themselves have learned not to cherish and hang onto these unworthy emotions. People with a keen sense of humor seldom seem moody. The sudden insight that produces humor seems to be favorable to a change of mood.

There is another insight that produces a lump in the throat and a tear in the eye. For lack of a better word, we will call this type of sudden insight "pathos." Sometimes, when all is dark, when all is hopeless, when all is evil, a sudden insight reveals some redeeming feature to us, and with this revelation comes the familiar lump in the throat and the tear in the eye.

This may be a transitional step out of depression. For example: Mary has lost a loved one through death. All seems dark and hopeless, and Mary sits numb and dry-eyed. Eventually there may come a sudden insight through which Mary will see some redeeming features. With this insight will come the tears, and Mary will take her first step out of this depressed mood.

The next time you sit through a tear-jerker in your local theater notice how these redeeming features produce the lump in your throat and the tears in your eyes. It may be that you suddenly realize, because of some redeeming feature, that the mean wife or mean husband is not so mean. Or in a situation where all seems evil there may appear some ray of good.

Johnny falls and skins his knee. It hurts like the dickens. Johnny's mother runs to him, picks him up and comforts him, thereby furnishing a redeeming feature to a bad situation—and Johnny yowls lustily.

Sometimes, through mental devices associated with our escape mechanisms, we imagine some redeeming feature that isn't there. For instance: Johnny may fall and bruise his knee when his mother is not near to comfort him. But, he remembers how she comforted him in a similar situation, he imagines her comforting him now, and so he wraps himself in a mantle of self-pity—and weeps.

Jane thinks the world is against her. "But they'll be sorry when I'm dead," she thinks. All of this sorrow that she imagines the world will feel for her is the redeeming feature, and she sobs in self-pity.

Self-pity is the most destructive of all our moods. Not only does it apply the brakes, bringing us to a standstill, but it may shove us into reverse. It may start us working against ourselves even to the point of self-destruction.

Sometimes a subtle sort of revenge prompts self-pity. We'll get even by making them feel sorry for us—sorry that they have ruined our lives or spoiled our fun. And so, viewing this imagined sorrow upon the part of others as a redeeming feature, we work against ourselves.

Again, a hopeless feeling of guilt may cause us to view self-destruction, degradation, failure, sickness, anything that can hurt us or bring us to ruin, as an atonement, and we see this atonement as a redeeming feature—hence the lump in the throat and the tear in the eye.

There is always the danger that such thoughts running through our mind in self-pity may result in some act of self-destruction. Psychiatrists believe that we may unconsciously seek to injure or destroy ourselves. They also believe that many psychosomatic disorders have their origin in self-pity.

The will-to-win melts like a lump of ice in the sun when we indulge in self-pity. We unconsciously see failure as an atonement of some sort and hence as a redeeming feature.

Self-pity is a weakness that none of us can afford to tolerate. As with any other mood, we must act promptly to stamp out the first few sparks. Once the mood is built, we are in somewhat the same situation as a bull wearing a pair of red sun glasses; everything the bull sees appears red.

Take the case of Helen and her child Betsy. A breakfast table argument between Helen and her husband leaves Helen in an angry mood. Her husband escapes to his office, leaving little

Betsy a victim to her mother's angry mood. Betsy squirms and wriggles as her mother ties the blue bow in Betsy's flaxen curls, dressing the child for school. Ordinarily Helen would smile with loving tolerance at all this wriggling, and perhaps hug Betsy to her as she lovingly pats the curls into place with the bow finally tied. But today Helen is in an angry mood. The quarrel at the breakfast table has made her sensitive to irritating stimuli and causes her to react angrily to stimuli that would not ordinarily irritate her. She slaps Betsy.

Betsy bursts into tears at this unexpected treatment. Her mother becomes even more irritated, and poor little Betsy will be fortunate if she escapes a sound whipping before she departs for school.

Your mood will influence your flying. For instance: If an airline pilot is involved in a lot of unsavory domestic trouble and leaves for work after he and his sparring partner have broken the family chinaware to bits, his efficiency as a pilot is likely to be impaired.

If he goes to work in an angry mood, he will be sensitive to all the stimuli that can irritate and anger him. Or, if he is involved in financial difficulties that make him feel insecure, he may approach his work in a fearsome mood, and any stimuli that can arouse fear and forebodings will attack him in full force.

If a flying student approaches his flying lesson in a critical mood, he is likely to blame his instructor or the airplane for his own faults, instead of making an attempt to remedy those faults.

Just as a radio is tuned to receive a definite program, a mood attunes us to a definite pattern of response to the stimuli of our environment.

A radio is a source of pleasure when we learn how to tune it to bring in the programs that we want. Our lives become effective as we learn how to foster moods characterized by patterns of response that lead us to our goals.

What Can We Do about Moods?

1.  Sometimes we can do as Hutchins did: we can avoid activities that are important to us when we are in a mood that cannot lead to effective action.

2.  We can halt the development of destructive moods by learning to recognize destructive emotions such as fear, hate, anger, rage, envy, and jealousy—stamping them out whenever they appear, before they have an opportunity to grow into a three-alarm fire.

3.  We can learn to recognize emotions of self-destruction that are characterized by self-pity, and stamp them out the moment they appear.

4.  We can take advantage of the reversibility of emotion.

We act > as we feel        We feel < as we act

The easiest way to stamp out an undesirable emotion is to plunge into constructive activity, either physical or mental. Physical activity seems the easiest.

5.  We can choose our social contacts with a view to acquiring the mood we desire, since we tend to absorb some of the mood of those with whom we associate. This is particularly true of mass gatherings. We develop a somber mood at a funeral, a gay mood at a wedding, and an aggressive mood at a patriotic rally. Or we may develop a violent mood if we are a party to a mob intent on a lynching.

6.  We can avoid fatigue where effective action is essential.

7.  We can avoid forebodings and worry since they lead to mental fatigue which, in turn, may foster a depressed mood.

8.  We can choose our reading matter with a view to inspiring the desired mood.

9.  We can choose music that inspires the desired mood.

10.  Even our manner of dress may affect our mood.

11.  Sometimes a good meal leads to a mood of contentment.

12.  As a last resort, drugs in the hands of a competent physician may be effective as an aid to changing a mood. For that matter a steaming cup of strong black coffee has been

known to lead to a surprising change in mood.

Our moods are like tides of life that tend to carry us in the direction in which they are surging. When these tides tend to carry us away from our goals, we are wise to resist them. If they tend to carry us in the direction of our goals, we can ride with them smoothly toward the fulfillment of these goals.

# 13
# The Psychology of Errors

Carl Sturgis, the man who taught me to fly, used words with great economy; he was short on giving advice. Yet I am convinced that I am alive today because of three simple words spoken by him.

It was easier for me to solve an intellectual problem than to master the reflexes so important to flying. I learned slowly, in a day when little time was devoted to flight training.

In those days ten hours of dual instruction, followed by one solo flight, constituted a complete course of instruction. That was before the days of aviation gasoline. We used what was known as stove and lighting gasoline, which came in fifty-five-gallon drums. Carl had it figured out that one of those drums held enough gasoline to operate the OX5 motor in the Curtis JN4D trainer for exactly ten hours.

As soon as a student laid the customary $500 on the line, Carl would point to a drum of gasoline on a rack and say, "That's what you've bought. There are ten hours of flying in that drum." We students made sure that the drums didn't leak.

I don't think Carl regarded me as the student most likely to succeed. In fact, I'm inclined to believe that he had some serious misgivings as to my future, for when we shook hands for the last time, as I was leaving school, he said, "Fly to live!" Then he added, "All that you hope to gain from flying will be lost if you die."

Those words echoed through my mind a great many times in the years that followed. When about to take off on some hazardous flight, I would always hear those words, "Fly to live!"

I was unlike the blind mule that the rascal sold to the trusting farmer. Later the farmer complained to him.

"That mule was blind. He walked right into a tree and

butted his brains out."

The rascal replied, "Hell! That mule could see good enough. He just didn't give a damn."

This "not giving a damn" is the cause of many accidents; rationalization—"It can't happen to me" and "I never make mistakes"—is another cause.

You are parked at the curb innocently studying a road map. You see the type of automobile sarcastically referred to by Easterners as the California Model coming down the street. It is nearly new but has undergone some drastic changes since it emerged from the factory. The four bashed-in fenders would never be recognized by the man who made them. The battered headlights are slightly askew, and the windshield is spider-webbed with splintered glass. The front bumper is hanging loosely by one support, and the radiator grill has long since disappeared.

You think, "Here comes a veteran of many traffic engagements. The scars of combat mark the driver as one of those persons who is always having an accident."

He is looking the other way as he nears you, and the front wheels of his car, jostled by a bump in the road, swerve his machine into a collision with your parked car.

You may be sure that he will jump out and hotly exclaim, "It was all your fault!" Such people are never wrong and always have a ready alibi.

A study of industrial accidents has revealed that there is a type of individual who is susceptible to accidents and has them regularly. The same is true in military life.

Black, the air safety officer of the Post, was demanding that his commanding officer ground Lt. Smith. The C.O. smiled tolerantly. "After all, Black, he only damaged the landing gear a little."

Black, however, was well armed with the facts. He hauled a stack of reports from his brief case. "Look!" he said, "he has had eleven of these minor accidents, three within the past two months, and he will keep right on having them."

"But, as you say," pointed out the C.O., "they are all minor accidents. He has never had a really serious accident of any kind."

"This long list of minor accidents proves he is the type of individual who is subject to accidents," insisted Black. "It's only a matter of time before he will have a serious accident. People like him always do."

"Nonsense!" rejoined the C.O. heatedly. "He's just been having a streak of bad luck. Call him in, give him a warning, and let it go at that. I can't afford to have him grounded when we need every available pilot."

Lt. Smith's streak of bad luck was not ended by a warning.

He raised his number of accidents to an even dozen with one that cost him his life. These accident types continue to have accidents because they never learn from experience. Either they refuse to accept responsibility, or they convince themselves that the responsibility does not lay on their shoulders, since "It can't happen to me—I never make any serious mistakes."

A major cause of accidents is the failure to realize the importance of details. A blacksmith welding a chain knows that each link must be perfect, that the chain is no stronger than its weakest link. This was vividly brought to my attention when I was serving in the Air Transport Command. Through a mix-up in paper work, I was once grounded for a month. During that month I was assigned to work in Operations, dispatching military aircraft.

The clearance form used had quite a few items to be filled in by the pilot and checked by the Operations Officer before he signed the clearance. I was soon signing twice as many clearances as any of the officers with whom I was working. Now and then one of my fellow officers, raising an eyebrow of disapproval, would remark, "You check those clearances pretty fast, don't you?" But that didn't bother me.

"They spend too much time checking unimportant details," I thought. "With all my flying experience I recognize

181

the important things and give minor details a quick glance."

I remember one clearance of which I was particularly proud when I signed it. The Lieutenant handed me a clearance from Palm Springs to Amarillo, Texas. He was flying an A-20, and I knew that an A-20 without a belly tank would be dangerously low on fuel before it reached Amarillo. I had flown a lot of A-20's over that same route.

I pointed this out to him. "Ever flown an A-20 before?" I asked. He admitted that he hadn't.

I looked at the weather sequence and I thought about that short runway he would have to land on at Winslow, with the wind in its present direction. I had landed a lot of A-20's on that runway, and I knew how short it was, so I said, "I'll clear you as far as Albuquerque on one condition: I want you to promise to check your fuel over Winslow, and if there is not enough to reach Albuquerque, with a good generous margin left over, or if thunderstorms in the mountains drift over onto your route, I want you to promise to land at Winslow."

He faithfully promised to comply with my wishes and I briefed him on the weather. Then with a quick glance over the remainder of the clearance, I signed it and sent him on his way.

The rank and duty of each member of the crew are supposed to follow his name on the clearance. There were two names at the top of the clearance, but neither rank nor duty was indicated opposite the second name on the clearance. I passed it over. These A-20's had a British radio that worked on a different set of frequencies than our own, and it was customary to assign a radio operator to each A-20.

Little did I realize that this omission on my part might endanger a valuable airplane and two lives. In fact, I smiled smugly to myself as I thought, "Those other officers would spend a lot of time checking unimportant little details like that, and maybe miss an important point like the gas capacity, or they might clear him to that short runway at Winslow." I glowed with pride in the efficient job I was doing.

That night, I was awakened by someone shaking my

shoulder. "Wake up! You're in trouble. That A-20 you dispatched to Albuquerque didn't arrive. It's four hours overdue. Its fuel is exhausted. It's down somewhere."

I hurried down to Operations. Major McFayden, my senior officer, in charge of Operations, glanced up from the maps he was studying and said, "It's a nasty mess. We'll have to organize a search party the first thing in the morning."

He swept his hand over a large mountainous area on the map. "They could be down anywhere in this area. God! we may not find the wreck for six months."

The Major understood men. He looked up again at me and said, "Don't take it too hard. It's really my responsibility. I should have warned you not to be in too big a hurry in signing clearances. You overlooked something important on that clearance. That A-20 was not equipped with the usual British radio and did not carry a radio operator. The second name on that clearance was an illegal passenger, and from what I've learned he wasn't wearing a parachute—you know what that means!"

I knew what it meant. The pilot would have to ride the plane down with his unfortunate passenger.

There wasn't an officer in the whole United States Army that I liked or respected more than Major McFayden, and I'd let him down. What he said was true. He was responsible for the mistakes made by men under him.

Around ten o'clock the next morning, we got the news that the pilot had safely crash-landed somewhere along the Rio Grande River, between El Paso and Albuquerque. The story trickled in:

He had plenty of gas left when he crossed over Winslow. Just before reaching Albuquerque, he encountered a thunderstorm. He detoured around it and found another storm blocking his path. He finally ended up hopelessly lost and running short of fuel.

He headed for a smooth, green meadow along the Rio Grande, and belly-ed the plane in—did a good job too. But our air safety officer had a way of getting to the bottom of things. He noted the absence of any indication of either rank or duty following the second name on the clearance. "The rank alone should have told you that this man was not a radio operator," he pointed out. "None of the radio operators assigned to those A-20's were commissioned officers."

After that it always seemed to take me just a little longer than my fellow officers to check a clearance. For one thing, I wanted to make sure that the duty and rank of each crew member were properly set down.

This contempt for minor details may spring either from the don't-give-a-damn attitude or from rationalizing. The overuse of any of the escape mechanisms is likely to introduce error into one's actions, since the escape mechanism is not a logical but an absurd association, based upon wishful thinking. Projection, for instance, can lead to error, as when one projects his frustration into his work, by smashing the very goal he is trying to achieve because the task becomes difficult for him.

Individuals who use the escape mechanisms to the point where a condition of mental illness exists are said to be neurotic or suffering from a neurosis.

Individuals who don't give a damn, who are utterly irresponsible, are said to be psychopathic personalities. It is believed that the habitual criminal is a psychopathic personality. You can become a reasonable facsimile of a psychopathic personality by an overindulgence in alcohol.

Physical causes for accidents and errors are to be found in fatigue, illness, excess worry, or depression.

Still more direct physical causes may be found in a lack of skill or in a lack of knowledge. However, one who is in good mental health and knows his own limitations can compensate for these physical shortcomings by using exceptional care. He is aware that these shortcomings may cause him to make an error. Such individuals profit from their past errors.

Neither the psychopathic personality nor the neurotic is likely to profit from past errors; they continue making the same mistakes. The psychopathic personality has little motivation to profit from past mistakes, since he just doesn't give a damn. The neurotic is not likely to profit from past mistakes because he places the blame for those mistakes somewhere other than with himself. If you find yourself blameless; if you know that you just don't make any mistakes; if you always have a ready alibi; if you know it is impossible for you to prevent the mistakes you make—then watch out —you're probably neurotic.

If, when a mistake is called to your attention you feel like saying, "So what! To hell with it! I don't give a damn! It's my neck, isn't it?" or some similar remark, you had better watch out too, for those are the earmarks of the psychopathic personality.

To sum up: Before considering the physical factors that enter into errors, it is well to understand the psychological factors, since one who suffers from either of these factors is not likely to profit greatly from an understanding of the physical factors. He either "just doesn't give a damn," or he never accepts the responsibility for his own mistakes but blames them on someone else, something else, or fate. Each type is irresponsible in his own peculiar way.

# 14

# When Death Strikes

Following each accident, the Air Force has a procedure for deciding where to place the error that made the accident possible. One hundred per cent pilot error was so common that we pilots used to say, "When you climb into an airplane you are making your first mistake and for that they give you 50 per cent pilot error. Then, when an accident occurs they simply add another 50 per cent and there you are—100 per cent pilot error."

Poor design of the airplane, mechanical or structural failures, weather, imperfect landing fields, the mistakes of other personnel, and even acts of God or coincidence do, of course, enter into most accidents. But when such factors by themselves need not have caused the accident, if the pilot had been on his toes, sufficiently resourceful, and endowed with the amount of skill that the qualified pilot is expected to possess, it is common practice to assess pilot error. It is a cold-blooded process for determining the most logical point at which to take some corrective measure.

Can you recall some happy Fourth of July when you, as a youngster of ten or eleven, were enjoying the festivities by firing off firecrackers? Then, in a careless moment, you allowed one to explode in your hand and, for you, the day was ruined.

Accidents have a way of marring our happiness and even our lives. Your dictionary has this to say about accidents: An event which was unexpected or the cause of which was unforeseen; a contingency, casualty, or mishap; a property of a thing which is not essential to it.

Let's go through that definition, starting with the last point. Accidents certainly are not an essential part of flying and they may be largely prevented by using care and foresight.

The definition itself suggests a remedy, since accidents are unexpected and unforeseen. By examining those accidents that have occurred we can learn to foresee what may happen under certain circumstances and learn to avoid those circumstances.

The Civil Aeronautics Authority conducts an investigation of each airplane accident and has tabulated the results. These records are extremely accurate. Painstaking care and honesty are observed by the investigators in drawing their conclusions. Suppose we examine a few of these reports to see what percentages of these accidents are due to pilot error.

PILOT ERRORS
Year
Total Number of Accidents (2nd column)
Accidents Caused Primarily by Pilot Error (3rd column)
Percentages of Accidents Due to Pilot Error (4th column)

| Year | Total Number of Accidents | Accidents Caused Primarily by Pilot Error | Percentages of Accidents Due to Pilot Error |
|---|---|---|---|
| 1945 | 4562 | 3441 | 73.9 |
| 1946 | 7618 | 4812 | 63.2 |
| 1947 | 9000 | 6012 | 66.8 |
| 1948 | 1000 | 675 | 67.5 |

The last line represents only the first 1000 accidents occurring in 1948. In 1945 the C.A.A. tabulated the various accidents as to cause, and we will briefly review this report.

BREAKDOWN OF PILOT ERRORS

| Cause of Accident | Total Number | Percentages of Fatal Accidents |
|---|---|---|
| Technique | 1490 | 4.4 |
| Judgment | 931 | 21.2 |
| Carelessness | 922 | 2.0 |
| Other pilot errors | 18 | 55.6 |

It will be noted that poor technique produced half again as many accidents as poor judgment, but that poor judgment produced nearly five times the number of fatalities.

Carelessness produced nearly as many accidents as poor judgment but was responsible for less than a tenth as many fatalities.

Other errors include mental unbalance and the use of alcohol and drugs. Although few in number, more than half were fatal.

It was further pointed out in this report that 41 per cent of the fatal accidents were the result of reckless, low, and show-off flying, together with the carrying of passengers by student pilots. Psychologically, such accidents are the result of neurotic or psychopathic tendencies—"I don't give a damn," or, "It can't happen to me—I don't make mistakes."

It is interesting to note that the accidents due to landing accounted for the highest percentage of those attributable to any one cause, whereas those due to forced landings constituted the second highest percentage. However, it should be carefully noted that the percentage of casualties involved was low for both of these types of accidents.

## TECHNICAL CAUSES FOR ACCIDENTS

|  | Per Cent | Per Cent Fatal |
|---|---|---|
| Landing | 33.5 | 1.3 |
| Forced landings | 20.4 | 2.7 |
| Taxiing | 12.7 | None |
| Collision with objects | 11.3 | 18.0 |
| Take-off | 9.4 | 1.6 |
| Stall-spin | 9.0 | 65.2 |
| Miscellaneous | 1.6 | 9.3 |
| Propeller accidents | 0.8 | 3.0 |
| Structural failures | 0.4 | 30.0 |
| Collision with other aircraft | 0.4 | 22.2 |
| Fire | 0.3 | |
| Undetermined | 0.2 | |

The stall-spin accidents occurred with great frequency, and, because of the high percentage of casualties carried by this type of accident, they produced more than half of the total number of fatalities. It would seem that more stress should be placed upon stalls and spins in training, and also that the pilot should realize that it is much more important to avoid stalling the airplane than to avoid the lesser damage from a poor landing. Many pilots are so intent on avoiding a landing mishap that they forget all about the hazard of the stall.

Collision with objects also took a high toll in fatalities, more than ten per cent of such accidents resulting in fatalities.

More than one-fourth of the forced landing accidents were those in which the forced landing occurred during the takeoff climb.

Four hundred and eight of the stall-spin accidents were found attributable to pilot error, and 138 were highlighted by reckless flying that culminated in the stall-spin. One-tenth of these accidents occurred during authorized acrobatic practice, many of which might have been avoided had the training been organized on an easy step-by-step progress basis with more time and thoroughness devoted to it. Ten per cent of the stall-spin accidents occurred in bad weather.

## A STUDY OF OBJECTS COLLIDED WITH

| Objects | No. of Accidents |
|---|---|
| Wires .................. | 218 |
| Trees .................. | 139 |
| Ground or water........ | 53 |
| Fences .................. | 37 |
| Mountains, hills......... | 19 |
| Poles .................. | 18 |
| Buildings ............... | 11 |

Wishful thinking in the form of rationalizing—"It can't happen to me" and "I don't make mistakes"—leads to many of these tragic mishaps.

A colored boy, walking through a cemetery, paused and looked thoughtfully at a tombstone that bore the following inscription: "Not dead—just sleeping." Finally he said, "You-all isn't kiddin' nobody but yusself."

190

When we indulge in wishful thinking as characterized by rationalizing, we are kidding no one but ourselves, and no pilot can afford to kid himself.

The men who fly our airlines are just about the best pilots in the business. Suppose we examine a few accidents in which these top pilots, with five thousand hours or more flying experience, have made errors that cost lives.

Shortly before 7:30, the morning of January 9, 1945, American Airlines Flight 6001 took off from La Guardia Airport, New York City, bound for the West Coast. Less than twenty-four hours later, at 1:45 the following morning, the last crew change was being made at El Paso, Texas. Passengers stirred restlessly in their seats, then dozed back to sleep again. Others peered out the windows to see the trim, thirty-eight-year-old pilot, who was to complete the flight, striding confidently out to the waiting airliner.

He had a right to be confident, with 6,315 flying hours tucked under his belt. He had been flying for American Airlines since 1940, as first officer until 1942 and, since then, as captain.

He frowned as he thought of the weather forecast for Burbank, his destination. The last sequence read: Overcast, ceiling 400 feet, visibility one mile, light fog till 12:30, followed by ceilings of 200 feet and visibility of i/£ mile, moderate fog, clouds stratus, top 1,800 feet.

"Looks like we'll have to land at Newhall," he said to his first officer. When Burbank was fogged-in, the airline used airports at either Newhall or Palmdale, since these airports, located on the rim of the desert, were seldom fogged-in.

Because of these weather conditions, the flight left El Paso cleared to Newhall, California. The tiresome hours of the night droned away. At 3:14 PST, they were approaching the two towering peaks which guard San Gorgonio Pass, the gateway to the desert. The captain tensed a little as he received the 3 A.M. special weather report for Burbank, which gave a measured ceiling of 700 feet, overcast, visibility 2 miles, with light fog.

His mind became alert as he planned for the instrument

let-down he would have to make at Burbank, in place of the contact landing at Newhall. He wasn't worried about the letdown; he had made it plenty of times in the past. But a pilot has to be mentally alert and on his toes during an instrument let-down, and this one looked a little doubtful to him.

Sure enough, six minutes later, the company advised him by radio that the flight had been re-cleared by the Los Angeles Air Traffic Control Center, to Burbank range station, to cross Burbank at 3,500 feet with no delay expected.

At 4:05 A.M., he was feeling his way down through the fog, his eyes alertly switching from instrument to instrument, and his ears alertly attuned to the radio range signals.

"I should have broken contact by this time," he muttered.

Less than a minute later he did break contact and saw the runway lights below him. "Missed our approach," he said to the co-pilot. "Might as well up the gear. We'll have to go to our alternate at Palmdale."

Had he stuck to that decision, I would not be writing this report, and the captain, his crew, and twenty-one passengers would be alive today.

Who knows, however, what passes through a man's mind on the brink of eternity? Perhaps, after he had descended a little lower and was passing over the end of the runway, the visibility looked a little better. Perhaps he thought, "Hell! No need to go to Palmdale. I can circle the airport beneath this damn soup and get in."

The fact that his gear was retracted when he passed over the end of the runway, as attested to by observers, is clear evidence that he had originally decided to turn to Palmdale, his alternate, since he would not have retracted the gear had he been planning to land at Burbank.

The traffic at Burbank is right-hand, but under conditions of low visibility pilots frequently call the tower and request permission to circle to the left, so that they may keep the airport clearly in view from the left seat.

"I'm alone in the traffic pattern," he thought, as he made

the turn, "no need to ask for permission."

The visibility became worse, and he lost sight of the runway lights. At 4:07 A.M., shortly after making the left turn, he radioed the control tower that he could not maintain contact and was proceeding to Palmdale, his alternate.

At this point he resorted to the standard missed-approach procedure, which calls for a right-hand climbing turn to a magnetic heading of 270 degrees, a climb to 3,500 feet, and a call to the company ground station for further instructions. But this missed-approach procedure can only be applied, at the very latest, when passing over the end of the runway. As we have seen, the pilot changed his mind at this point. Now he was committed to another course of action. He could have stuck to it. He could have timed each leg of the rectangular pattern that would lead him around to the runway. He could have maintained such a procedure, even after losing contact through poor visibility.

However, in the indecisive moment when he decided to circle the airport instead of using the missed-approach procedure, he no doubt neglected to check the time at which he turned. A timing of the legs of the rectangle was now denied him, and it would be hazardous to circle blind without the aid of such timing.

His mind instantly reverted to the missed-approach procedure which he had originally intended to use. He began making a right-hand turn to a heading of 270 degrees.

Now, however, he was near the hills, and there was insufficient room to complete the turn from this point. At about 4:50 A.M., the C.A.A. was notified that the aircraft had missed its approach and had not been heard from since.

At 9:30 A.M., the wreckage was sighted on a hillside about 23/4 miles northeast, and at an altitude of about 1,034 feet above the level of the airport.

In its report, the Civil Air Board, which investigated the accident, gave as the probable cause: "The pilot attempted to use the standard missed-approach procedure after having followed another course to a point where it was impossible to apply this procedure safely."

When the captain switched from his original decision to use the missed-approach procedure, he switched to a procedure for which he had no adequate plan, otherwise he could have safely followed through on the new decision. This is the deadly factor involved in changing one's mind. One is likely to adopt a procedure which he has not planned, with the result that this too fails to work out, and he must, as this pilot did, change from this course too. Then he makes his last decision so hastily that he overlooks a bit of important data, just as this pilot failed to recognize that he could not safely use the missed-approach procedure from the point at which he now found himself.

Place yourself in his position at the moment of that last fatal decision. You are headed for the hills and you have lost contact through poor visibility. You are flying blind, do not know your exact position, and have no means of quickly discovering where you are. You must do something at once or you will crash into those hills ahead. You can turn in one of two directions, either to the right or to the left. Since the missed-approach procedure—the safe way out when you miss an approach—calls for a right-hand turn, wouldn't you too have turned to the right?

Before reporting on the next disaster I am going to recount a couple of slips that I once made, which were of much the same nature as the one that caused trouble for a pilot taking off from La Guardia Airport.

This flying is a fast business—people are always trying to hurry a pilot—and a pilot cannot afford to allow himself to be hurried.

A thirty-mile-an-hour gusty wind was blowing at Tucson that morning as I taxied the B-17 out to the end of the runway, with the gust-locks holding the control surfaces from being buffeted by the strong wind. We ran up the engines and completed our pre-take-off check and I radioed the tower, asking for take-off clearance. Both the co-pilot and myself leaned over to release the gust-lock on the elevator and rudder controls, which is accomplished by releasing a lever so that it falls to the floor under spring tension.

Just then the tower barked in my ears, "Army 561, you are cleared for immediate take-off or to hold. There is an airplane turning on final approach."

I didn't want to have to wait for this airplane to land and clear the runway. I grasped the four throttles and began sliding them open. By the time I was lined up with the runway we were rolling ahead under full power.

Then I booted the controls to make sure that they were operating freely. The wheel would not turn. In my haste to get under way, I had failed to remove the pin that locked the ailerons. I managed to ease the controls ahead and to grasp the red knob pulling the pin free on the run, but my co-pilot and I shot a significant glance at each other.

Another time I was cleared on instruments from Patterson Field, at Dayton, Ohio, to Mitchell Field, Long Island. I was flying a B-24 that was equipped with what we called a "hot-wing," in place of the regular rubber de-icing boots. I was a little anxious about that hot-wing. I knew that I would encounter severe icing conditions on my flight to Mitchell Field, and it did not comfort me to recall that the man who had designed the hot-wing had been killed in an accident during the testing of the wing. I wondered.

At the end of the runway I ran up my engines, made my pre-take-off check, and asked the tower for take-off clearance. I was just completing the pre-take-off check when the tower advised, "B-24, your instrument clearance to Mitchell Field has been approved by Air Traffic Control. For your information, there is a formation of planes approaching the airport, the first plane of which is now turning on final approach. Unless you can take off at once, your take-off will be delayed indefinitely. You are cleared for immediate take-off or to hold."

In the original cockpit check, one makes a careful check of each detail. It has been my custom to make a quick pre take-off recheck of important details. In my hurry to get going, I neglected to make this final check.

I rolled onto the runway and applied full power. The air-speed indicator crept up to take-off speed, but we did not rise from the runway. I began rolling the elevator trim tab. The nose rose a little, but still the plane did not leave the runway. We were well beyond the speed normally required for take-off, yet still glued to the runway.

It was then that I glanced down at the flap indicator and saw that I had neglected to lower my flaps, and this heavy B-24—it was a special radar job—needed flaps for a quick take-off. Fortunately, I had a runway 7,680 feet long and had plenty of time to lower my flaps and get into the air.

As I make this next report of an accident that snuffed out forty-three lives, because a pilot forgot something, on a runway only 3,530 feet long, I cannot help but feel, "Save for the grace of God, that could have been me."

The captain of United Airlines Flight 521 prepared his instrument flight plan between La Guardia Airport and Cleveland, Ohio, with his customary care. The giant four-rnotored Douglas Transport was to be loaded with 48 human beings, including himself. He noted that, according to the forecast, a prefrontal squall line with thunderstorm conditions would break over La Guardia at 7 P.M. He was not alarmed by this condition, as he was scheduled to depart from La Guardia at 6:40 P.M.

The first of those little seemingly inconsequential events that were to add up to tragedy occurred when the time of departure was set back to 7 P.M., because of a delay in servicing and loading the airplane.

At 6:55, the captain began taxiing out to the north end of runway 18, the shortest runway at La Guardia Airport. Adjacent to the end of the runway he made his customary engine run-up and take-off check. Because of the gusty wind that was blowing he taxied out and made his engine run-up and take-off check with the gust-locks applied, to prevent buffeting of the controls by the wind.

At the end of the take-off check he released the gust-locks, as was his custom, and it became the duty of his first officer, commonly referred to as the co-pilot, to hold the controls against the buffeting of the wind, while the captain radioed the tower for permission to take off.

At this point another little event contributed its share to the chain of events leading to disaster. He was held up for six or seven minutes because of a difference between him and Airway Traffic Control, with reference to his instrument clearance, which had to be straightened out before his departure.

Meanwhile, black thunder clouds and lightning were visible west of La Guardia. The squall line was breaking over Hell Gate, some two or three miles to the west of La Guardia.

While the captain gazed apprehensively at the approaching thunderstorm and fumed over the delay, his co-pilot, tiring of the struggle to hold the controls against the wind, applied the gust-locks again, intending to release them before take-off.

At 7:04, the captain advised the tower that Flight 521 was ready for take-off. The tower operator asked whether the flight wished to wait out the approaching storm on the ground. The captain replied, "I'll take off."

The tower then advised the captain, "You are cleared for immediate take-off or to hold, traffic on final approach north of Riker's Island." The final sequence of events leading to disaster had fallen into place.

Flight 521 taxied from its parked position, rolled onto runway 18, and without pause or hesitation, accelerated for take-off. The co-pilot, aware of the captain's impatience and the urgency for haste, gave his full attention to the application of power, forgetting all about the gust-locks.

The airspeed indicator crept up to 90 miles an hour. As the captain applied pressure to the controls he found that they had a heavy feel and that the aircraft did not respond. The memory of releasing the gust-locks was so clear that he did not connect the difficulty with the gust-lock mechanism.

He was not aware that the co-pilot had reapplied the gust-locks, and the co-pilot, busy with his other duties, was not aware of the captain's problem and did not remember about the gust-locks.

Finally, the captain signaled the co-pilot to cut off the power. At about 1,000 feet from the end of the runway the captain applied the brakes, attempting a ground-loop by the heavy application of the left brake. The airplane refused to be detoured from disaster, proceeding straight ahead over the end of the runway to crash through the fence. It half flew across the Grand Central Parkway, and finally came to rest about 800 feet beyond the end of the runway, just east of the Casey Jones School of Aeronautics.

It was immediately enveloped in flames. The captain and four other occupants of the plane escaped with their lives. The other 43 occupants, including the co-pilot, perished.

The Civil Air Board which investigated the accident gave as the probable cause: "The inability of the pilot to actuate the controls due to the gust-locks being on, resulting in the pilot's decision to discontinue the take-off at a point too far down the runway to permit stopping within the boundaries."

It is possible that the captain himself may have reapplied the gust-locks and then forgotten to remove them. This seems extremely unlikely since, had he done so, he would most surely have thought of the gust-locks when he discovered that the controls were inoperative, and a mere tap, a split-second reflex act on his part, would have released them.

Furthermore, the captain has steadfastly insisted that the gust-locks were not on during the take-off, which would naturally be his opinion if he definitely remembered releasing the gust-locks and was unaware that his co-pilot had applied them again.

The captain, however, was operating on some exceedingly fine margins, which brings to mind the story of the Irishman who was always wishing that he knew the exact spot where he was going to die. When one of his friends asked him what good such knowledge would be to him, he replied, "Faith and begorrah and I'd nivver go near the damn spot." If pilots would refuse to go near the spot where accidents occur, about 90 per cent of the fatal accidents could be prevented.

This spot where 90 per cent of the fatal accidents occur is the situation wherein the pilot operates in marginal conditions. Runways that are barely long enough—or not quite long enough. Airplanes loaded to the hilt—or a little beyond. Flights with just enough fuel for their completion—or not quite enough. Flights through weather at the minimums— or just a trifle below.

When more than one marginal condition exists, the pilot is using good judgment if he refuses to take off; these marginal conditions have a way of ending in disaster. When the margins are thin, it doesn't take much of the unexpected to produce an accident, and when a great many marginal conditions exist there are so many points where the unexpected may turn up that one is courting disaster to conduct an operation under such conditions.

Let's see how many marginal conditions the captain of this airliner faced on this ill-fated flight:

1. The runway was barely long enough.

2. The runway had a slight uphill grade, being ten feet higher at the far end than at the end from which the take-off was started.

3. There was a 32-foot obstruction at the end of the runway, which still further reduced the margin of safety.

4. The airplane was loaded to the hilt, and there was considerable question as to whether it was not actually over-leaded, especially in view of the short distance available for take-off on this particular runway.

5. The approaching storm made a wind-shift likely. In the event of the wind shifting to the tail of the airplane, a much greater distance would be required for take-off.

Had the pilot been taking off on a longer runway, he

would have had time to analyze his difficulty. He would undoubtedly have discovered that the gust-locks were on and, by a mere tap of the operating mechanism, could have released them. As it was, with the plane within a thousand feet of the end of the runway, and with the 32-foot obstruction staring him in the face, he had no choice but to make an attempt to stop the airplane.

We can list the unforeseen factors that added up to cause this tragic accident:

1. The delay in loading the airplane. Had it not been for this delay the pilot would have taken off as planned, well in advance of the approaching storm.

2. The second delay while the matters pertaining to the clearance were being adjusted. The gust-locks would not have been applied the second time had it not been for this second delay.

3. The fact that the pilot was hurried because another airplane was entering the final approach. He had either to get going or to hold until the other airplane had completed its landing and had cleared the runway. This hurrying no doubt was responsible for the fact that the gust-locks were overlooked.

4. A windshift could have contributed to the accident by still further narrowing the margins and also by increasing the difficulties encountered in bringing the giant plane to a stop short of disaster.

Eliminate any one of these unforeseen incidents and there would have been little likelihood of an accident. It was the captain's—and the passengers'—misfortune that they all added up to disaster. That is why it is dangerous to operate on thin margins.

A pilot reasons that he can safely carry out an operation within such narrow margins, but he does not take the unexpected into consideration. In this case the pilot was confronted with not one but with four unexpected incidents.

Let's check the points at which a different action might have prevented the accident.

1. There was a longer runway available although it would have entailed a take-off slightly crosswind. The use of this longer runway might well have saved the day, despite all the unforeseen incidents.

2. The pilot might have elected to wait out the storm on the ground instead of hurrying to get off ahead of the airplane which was approaching the airport for a landing. This choice would unquestionably have prevented the accident.

Either of these choices would have widened the margins of the operation to a point where there was little likelihood of an accident.

Many pilots cannot see the need for wide margins of safety in the operation of aircraft. They are capable. They know just what to do and have the necessary skill with which to do it successfully. They feel sure nothing can possibly happen. But they have overlooked the unforeseen. The wider margins provide the latitude whereby they can successfully encounter the unforeseen.

Next, we will consider an accident in which the pilot, by wishful thinking, convinced himself that he could make a flight when the weather was below the minimum for contact flight, despite the fact that he planned to land at an airport that was not set up for an instrument let-down.

"Should I pass up Morgantown?" It was the captain of Pennsylvania Central's Flight 142 asking the question.

The Flight Advisory Service of the C.A.A. at Pittsburgh answered, "There is a cold front in the vicinity of Morgan-town. The ceiling will lower to below the minimum behind the front."

Since Morgantown was not set up for an instrument letdown, the flight into Morgantown would have to be contact. However, this pilot rationalized, "I don't make any serious errors. Nothing will happen to me. I'll fly half-contact and half-instrument and get away with it."

He departed from Pittsburgh at 4:41, on the 14th day of April, 1945. He had cleared with a cruising altitude of 2,500 feet. The minimum altitude established for the route was 3,300 feet, a wise precaution for such instrument flights, since the highest mountain in the entire state of Pennsylvania lies just off the airway to the east.

The captain was making a sort of half-instrument and half-contact flight. He was cleared for instrument flight, but intended to land at an airport that was not set up for an instrument approach. Thus, it was necessary that he maintain contact, since an instrument let-down at Morgantown was out of the question. He planned to fly low enough so that he might catch occasional glimpses of the ground and would be able to recognize the airport at Morgantown by visual references, yet much of the time he would be in the soup, actually flying on instruments. Observers who saw the airliner on its ill-fated flight stated that it was continually in and out of the overcast.

Now the captain was well aware that this type of flying was not only contrary to regulations, but that it was regarded as exceedingly foolhardy. He must have rationalized, "It can't happen to me"—but unfortunately it did.

The principal error lay in attempting to land at Morgantown when weather conditions made such a procedure unsafe, especially when it would involve the violation of C.A.A. regulations, designed to maintain safe operations. The flight was exceedingly foolhardy in view of the fact that, at the time, the dew point was just one degree below the temperature, which meant that a temperature drop of a single degree might produce fog.

However, if he was determined to ignore regulations and make the flight, the captain would have been safer making the flight in good old Cub style. Since the minimums were below those required for a contact flight, this also would have broken the rules, but it would have carried less of a hazard. Apparently the pilot believed that the irregularity in his clearance would not be noticed and that it would be less of a violation to straddle the fence. He would try to maintain some semblance of a well-ordered instrument flight, but at an illegal altitude that would enable him to get occasional glimpses of the terrain below, which was essential if he were to land at Morgantown.

He flew at 2,500 feet, continually in and out of the clouds. He apparently believed that he could maintain his course from occasional glimpses of the Monongahela River, which occasional breaks in the irregular cloud deck permitted.

At Brownsville, the river veers slightly to the west of the course. It seems likely that the captain believed that he could sight the river again at the following side of bend, when it again paralleled his course. He took a short cut, no doubt checking with the beam at the same time.

Apparently the next glance he caught of a river from a hole in the cloud deck was the Cheat River, which he mistook for the Monongahela. After he lost sight of the Monongahela, at the point where it flowed westward in a sweeping bend, he may inadvertently have steered a little to the left of his course, possibly in following the radio range signals. Or the wind may have drifted him a bit to the left so that he made the error of mistaking the Cheat River for the Monongahela River and proceeded to use it as a visual reference to guide his flight.

His course, using the Cheat River as a reference, took him still farther to the left until, at 5 P.M., he was in the vicinity of Cheat Mountain. Just slightly less than twenty minutes after his take-off from Pittsburgh he crashed near the top ridge, on the west side of Cheat Mountain, at an elevation of about 2,100 feet, and about seven miles east-northeast of the Morgantown Airport; approximately seven miles off course and two miles off the airway.

Severed tree tops indicated that the plane was in a descent of about 300 feet per minute and was banked slightly to the right at the moment of impact. In view of the fact that the pilot crashed at an elevation four hundred feet below that at which he had been flying, it seems likely that he belatedly recognized his position and was turning and letting down for the approach to the Morgantown Airport.

The plane burst into flames which destroyed it and its twenty occupants. Twenty people died because a pilot was in the overcast at an altitude that was contrary to the regulations designed to make flying safe. He rationalized, "Such regulations are not meant for me. They are for pilots who lack my super-ability and genius for flying. I never make any mistakes—it can't happen to me." He made several errors, and it did happen to him.

That is how death comes to the best men who fly. The same factors are even more deadly to the less experienced pilot with less skill, and who is more likely to make errors in a moment of panic. We think, "I don't panic," but accidents caused by panic happen every day.

Panic, as it applies to the airplane pilot in many situations, is merely a natural adaptive response—the intense desire to flee to a point of security when confronted with danger. The most logical point of security is obviously the earth. He is motivated by a desire to get safely on the ground—and quickly.

In case of motor failure or some condition growing progressively worse, this desire to reach ground safely is often a worthy motive, but even then the flight to security cannot be too precipitant or it may lead to errors that end by placing the airplane on the ground in a crumpled heap. To reach the ground safely and intact, it is necessary to proceed in a step-by-step procedure, in an orderly manner, which is made easier by a clear understanding of the problem and the methods for its solution.

There are many occasions when the pilot may be more secure if he remains in the air and carefully surveys and analyzes the situation before acting.

Jonathan Eeds sat hunched forward in the cockpit of his little Cub monoplane, staring at the dark clouds in the sky ahead and the gray curtain of dust swirled up by the approaching squall. The throttle was pushed to its limits and possibly bent a little beyond. His body was tensed as though he were trying to aid the efforts of the motor.

He was beginning to wish he had given more thought to the weather forecaster's warnings of possible thunderstorms at his destination. He was only a few miles from Mt. Hawley Airport and he was racing madly ahead to beat the approaching thunderstorm to the landing field.

As he reached the airport, puffs of dust were already beginning to swirl obliquely across the field and he could see a wall of descending rain just beyond. The wind sock was viciously whipping up and down, darting from side to side, twisting like some huge serpent in mortal agony, but he breathed a prayer of thanks. The wind, according to the wind sock, was on his nose so that he could go straight in without circling the airport.

He cut the motor and nosed the little monoplane into a dive against the driving wind that was carrying great drops of rain which splattered on the windshield. The wind buffeted him up and down and he fought to keep the wings level and the little Cub on a straight approach to the runway.

Just as he felt the wheels touch the ground, a heavy gust picked up the right wing. Up-up-up it went, despite his efforts to control it, until the left wing hit the ground. The little, yellow monoplane seemed to hesitate for an instant, then cartwheeled over on its back, with a rending, crunching, tearing crash—then silence, save for the shriek of the wind.

It might have been worse. The little monoplane was pretty well demolished, but Jonathan escaped injury. A few seconds later and he might have been caught in a blinding torrent of rain and might have stalled out or dived into the ground.

Twenty minutes later the storm had passed, and a crowd of spectators was prying and poking through the crumpled wreck of Jonathan's airplane. The wind sock was hanging down at an angle of forty-five degrees in the gentle breeze now blowing, and the sun was peeping out from the clouds above. All was peaceful.

Had Jonathan flown off to one side and waited twenty minutes while the storm passed, he could then have come in for a safe landing. Better still, he might have turned back and returned to an airport that he had passed over some ten minutes previous to the crash, to land and wait out the storm in safety. The wise pilot always carries a plentiful reserve of fuel to enable him to circumvent such emergencies as this.

Impatience to get on the ground at night or at the end of a tiring, grueling flight, or impatience to beat other aircraft to a landing when circling an airport amid heavy traffic, has caused the needless loss of many airplanes and not a few lives.

"The air forgives no mistakes," was one of the earliest maxims of flying. No friendly judge to soften the sentence. No governor to pardon the offender. And no allowance for good behavior. The air is no respecter of persons. It will crack down on the worthy and unworthy alike when they make mistakes, and there is no allowance made for ignorance. Your first mistake may bring as severe a penalty as any other.

It's different now. You can make two mistakes. For the past twenty years, competent government agencies have studied the causes of accidents with the purpose of devising means for their prevention. The rules and regulations set up by these agencies are for the protection of the pilot and all who fly. They are like the signs that warn a skater to beware of thin ice. There is little likelihood that a single error can bring disaster when you observe rules and regulations.

The individual who does not obey the rules often places himself in a situation where one tiny slip, one little error, can cause his death.

I have carefully leafed through the reports of accident investigations by the C.A.A. and the C.A.B. and have been amazed to discover that in almost every instance some rule or regulation had been broken during the flight which ended in disaster, and in more than half of the cases such a violation led directly to the disaster or contributed to such an extent that it was obvious that the accident would not have occurred had it not been for the violation of the rules and regulations.

It is gratifying to all who love the game to observe how safe flying has become. Yet, three fourths of the fatal accidents that do occur could be prevented if the rules and regulations were heeded. In effect, the government agencies have provided a cut-and-dried formula for flying, the use of which will eliminate three fourths of the accidents. Unfortunately, many pilots rationalize as follows:

1. "I know pilots should not indulge in show-off flying, it's too dangerous—but not for me. I'm such a hot-shot that nothing can happen to me—I don't make mistakes."

2. "I know the rules have been formulated through years of careful study to protect me—but I don't need any protection—I can get by without the rules—I'm not subject to errors."

3. "I know a pilot shouldn't fly when ill, or when suffering from excess fatigue, but that doesn't apply to me—I'm so far superior to other pilots and besides it can't happen to me—it just can't."

4. "I know bad weather gets the best of them—but not me—I'm just too good a pilot to get caught and besides such a thing just couldn't happen to a guy like me."

Sounds silly doesn't it? Yet that is often the way you and I unconsciously feel.

As men grow older they normally acquire better judgment, and such judgment causes them to obey the rules. Perhaps that is the reason for the odd fact brought out by another C.A.A. analysis of accidents.

In this analysis it was discovered that a pilot's safety record improves until he has reached the age of 55. The analysis revealed that during instruction the safety records of pilots between the ages of 40 to 45 were nearly five times as good as the safety records of those between the ages of 20 to 25. A study of automobile accidents has revealed much the same situation. In fact, some insurance companies will not write automobile insurance for the younger group of drivers because of their high accident rate.

There is nothing smart or admirable about breaking the rules. Quite the contrary: The good sportsman observes the rules that govern any sport in which he indulges. To obey the rules is the sign of mature, sound judgment, the mark of the individual who is in sound mental health and has learned to adapt successfully to his environment.

One airline is giving applicants for pilot jobs a cunning psychological examination. One part of the examination is designed to determine by means of disguised questions and tests whether or not the individual is what psychologists call the accident type.

Prominent among these questions are those designed to discover whether the applicant is a psychopathic personality, one of these individuals who just doesn't give a damn—and cheerfully proceeds to break all rules.

The school of thought that believes that such don't-give-a-damn personalities possess such a lack of fear that they perform better in tight spots is rapidly taking a back seat. Not only do they get into more tight spots but they lack the intelligent judgment to get out of them safely. All we can say for them is that they are quick to act—often wrong.

# 15

# The Psychology of Buck Fever and Checkitis

The zest of autumn is in the air. Through the bright, colored woods, a man dressed in a red jacket and a red cap, and carrying a new gun, is cautiously poking his way.

Suddenly he tenses as he sees a huge buck in front of him. His hands tremble with excitement as he flings the gun awkwardly to his shoulder. His gaze is riveted to the magnificence of the animal. Already he can see those beautiful antlers gracing a space above the fireplace in his home. He has but one thought—to squeeze the trigger quickly before the buck gets away, for it has already started to run.

Somehow he can't get the gun butt snuggled firmly against his shoulder. Once the butt of the gun is securely in contact with his shoulder, he can't find the buck in the sights, and the gun barrel wavers in a maddening circle as he tries to line up the buck. Finally, he momentarily accomplishes this difficult feat and squeezes the trigger.

He finds that the trigger is a solid bit of metal that refuses to budge—because he has forgotten to release the safety catch.

He releases the safety catch, and with wild haste goes through the whole performance again, in an even more clumsy attempt. By this time the buck is actually out of range, but he hastily squeezes the trigger when he finally catches a fleeting glimpse of the animal in the line of his gun-sights.

How differently the experienced hunter acts. First he carefully releases the safety catch. He snuggles the gun firmly and comfortably to his shoulder, bringing the gun barrel up in a deliberate, searching manner, so that the buck quickly appears in the sights. Then he squeezes the trigger, and the chances are that those beautiful antlers will be added to the collection over

209

his fireplace.

He has been through this before. Sure, he is anxious to get the buck, but he doesn't allow his anxiety to hurry any of the steps directed toward attaining that end. He keeps his attention directed to each step in turn, until when he reaches the final step, toward which each previous step has been leading, he is in a position to make that final step effective.

The inexperienced hunter is defeated by his overanxiety to get the buck. He is afraid there isn't time enough to act before the buck gets out of range. He hurries each step so that it is poorly executed. Instead of keeping his attention on the step he is performing, he is way ahead, thinking of future steps. No wonder he fumbles awkwardly and forgets to release the safety catch.

That is one reason why experience is so helpful. The individual with experience knows just about how much time he can allot to each step; he is not so likely to hurry any step. He keeps his attention on what he is doing instead of on what he will soon be doing.

Previous success builds confidence. But even men with confidence may suffer from buck fever; because of their anxiety to get the job done quickly, they hurry through the early steps, until they are in no position to make the final step effective.

The easy way to master buck fever is to:

1. Know your problem, how long it takes to complete it, and the amount of time to allot to each step.

2. Master each step so that you may effectively accomplish it and know how long it takes to do so.

3. Use care not to hurry the early steps; keep your mind on what you are doing.

Buck fever is a condition where over anxiety causes one to direct his attention to an attempt to solve a problem in one great leap instead of in an easy step-by-step process.

Buck fever may stem from two kinds of feeling:

1. The feeling that the problem is so important that it must be solved quickly, with the result that his attention is

directed more to the problem itself than to each step in its turn.

2. The feeling that there is insufficient time to complete the problem causes one to hurry, with the result that he is not able to keep his attention directed to the various steps as he performs them.

Buck fever is often a combination of these two feelings. One of my army experiences which I seldom mention furnishes a good example of buck fever.

When I entered the Air Transport Command, a month after Pearl Harbor, I had some 15,000 flying hours, 7,651 of which were logged and more than 1,500 of which were on multi-engined equipment. I was soon flying four-engined bombers.

The Air Transport Command had established a policy requiring all four-engine pilots to hold an instrument rating. When it was discovered that I did not possess an instrument card, I was promptly ordered to an instrument school.

Unfortunately for me, someone must have assumed that since I was flying four-engined equipment I also had a lot of instrument flying experience even though I did not possess the card. I was sent to an advanced instrument school, where it was assumed that the pilot already possessed the white card, the course being designed for polishing his instrument flying and putting on the final touches to prepare him for the green instrument card, which is the highest instrument rating awarded.

When the captain who was assigned to instruct me learned that, despite my many hours of contact flying, I did not have any instrument experience and had never even been in a Link Trainer, he promptly took me to see the major.

He finished his remarks to the major in no uncertain terms, saying, "You know as well as I do that he hasn't the chance of a snowball in hell of getting through this course."

The major frowned. "I know it," he said, "but he has been ordered to the school and we have no choice but to run him through the course, flunk him out, and return him to his post."

I did flunk the course and several similar courses which

followed it.

By the time I had reached my fifth instrument school, I knew the facts of instrument flight. I fully understood the problem but I could not successfully complete an instrument let-down. I invariably fouled up somewhere during those fleeting seven minutes.

It seemed to me that there were so many things to do in the seven minutes of an instrument let-down that I didn't have time to do them and still keep the airplane within the limitations of fifty feet longitudinally, and within three degrees directionally, as was required to pass the instrument check.

One day a friendly flight surgeon who had heard of my difficulties became interested in my case and called me in for a conference.

He grinned pleasantly. "I'm going to make an instrument pilot out of you."

Enjoying my startled look of amazement, he continued, "I mean it! I have a little pill here that will do the trick."

He tossed the pill into the air and caught it in his hand, then laid it on the desk between us. Turning to face me, he said, "I believe you have convinced yourself that there is insufficient time in the seven minutes of a let-down to accomplish all that you have to do. Your instructor tells me that you have mastered each step so that you can execute it with precision but that when you start on the let-down a change comes over you. You work feverishly, fumbling along until, finally, somewhere during those seven minutes, you always manage to foul the whole thing up.

"You are so anxious to make it, and so afraid that you haven't time, that you don't keep your mind on what you are doing."

He pointed to the pill lying on his desk. "This pill contains a potent dose of an extremely powerful stimulant to the central nervous system. It speeds the mental processes and produces a feeling of confidence with no impairment to judgment. Being aware that your mental processes are working faster, you may not be so anxious about time—those seven minutes may seem more like fourteen. You will be able to keep your mind on each step as you come to it and do a nice job."

I remember grinning sheepishly and saying, "I suppose this is some psychological trick, but I'm for it if it will help me."

"There is no trick to it, as you will recognize once you take the pill," he replied. "Take it about an hour before take-off time for your next instrument flight, for it takes about thirty minutes to an hour for it to take full effect."

When we landed that afternoon after my regular instrument lesson, my instructor was beaming with pleasure. "Well! What's happened to you? I've never seen such a fine job of instrument flying. Your let-down could not have been improved in any way. If it wasn't for the fact that you have been doing such lousy work, I would send you up for your check ride tomorrow. Fly like this just two more times in a row, just to prove to me that it is not an accident, and I will send you up for that check ride."

He kept his word, and three days later I was taking off for my check ride in a B-24. The B-24 is not an easy airplane to fly on instruments, but since I had been doing such lousy work all through the course, and also because I was flying B-24's a great deal, it was thought wise to give me my check in the B-24.

I took the little white pill that the flight surgeon had given me that morning and climbed confidently into the left-hand seat of the B—24. It was not until we were in the air that I realized that the flight surgeon had double-crossed me, and I understood his reason for doing so. He had slipped me a Placebo. A Placebo is a pill that looks just like the one to which you are accustomed but is made of some inert substance that produces no effect whatever.

I passed the test with little difficulty. During the let-downs made with the aid of the magic pill, I came to realize that there was plenty of time to take care of each and every detail during those trying seven minutes.

I kept my mind on each step as I came to it and didn't

worry about the final step. Incidentally, I have never since felt any need for the magic pill. All that the pill accomplished was to prove to me that I had plenty of time and that I could do all that was necessary, with ease.

Checkitis is a condition in which one tries to act as he thinks someone wants him to act, instead of using his own initiative. He has picked a false goal. He's trying to pass a check ride instead of trying to do a good, capable job of flying.

During the early days of World War II, a great many competent, experienced pilots were drawn into the Air Transport Command. These men did not lack skill or confidence. Yet they often put on a poor performance during transition.

It was customary to give a pilot an hour or more of transition training when he was about to advance to another type of airplane. Many of these old hands were so anxious to please their instructor, who in many cases had less than a quarter of the amount of their flying experience, that they badly bungled this transition training.

The instructors in transition were often puzzled by the extremely competent manner in which these pilots handled their job once they got past transition, whereas many of the younger pilots, fresh out of cadet school, sailed smoothly through transition only to meet with disaster when they were strictly on their own.

These old hands were competent, but in transition they tried to fly as they believed their transition instructors wanted them to fly, instead of acting on their own initiative. They failed to realize that a good job of flying was all that was needed to please their instructors. Perhaps this was greatly augmented by the fact that these old pilots seemed to feel that their instructors neither approved of them nor of their style of flying.

They would try to figure out how the transition instructor wanted them to fly and often waited for some hint from the instructor before they acted. Often they would do just the opposite of what they normally would have done in the same circumstances had they been on their own. They seemed to believe that there were three ways of doing a thing: the right way, the wrong way, and the army way.

Many students are extremely difficult to teach because they are so inordinately anxious to please their instructor that they are unable to direct their attention to just doing a good job of flying, secure in the knowledge that such an accomplishment could not fail to please the instructor.

Such individuals, instead of reacting to stimuli in a natural manner, stifle awareness of those things vital to flying, by directing their attention to an attempt to become aware of what the instructor is thinking. It is difficult to put on a good performance if one must run all his thoughts through someone else's mind as well as his own.

Checkitis is actually a substitution of a false goal that takes the attention away from the real goal. The individual taking a check ride has the feeling that the important thing is to please the person who is giving him the check. This can be attained only by doing a good job of flying, which is the real goal.

Suppose a pilot is doing a simulated forced landing. When the motor is cut, he has a problem—he must get the airplane safely on the ground. He immediately noses the airplane down, to maintain flying speed, and searches the terrain below for the most likely spot on which to land. Once he has selected this spot, he maneuvers the airplane so that he can approach the spot at just the right altitude and with the correct amount of speed for a landing. Since, with a dead engine, he cannot regain either altitude or speed, without sacrificing the other, he maintains a slight reserve of altitude and speed which he maneuvers to lose just before the final leveling off.

He performs in the most direct, easy manner possible to accomplish these ends, just as he would do if he were alone with a dead engine. He is secure in the knowledge that the performance itself is the only thing that really matters. He may even forget that there is a critic watching his performance.

Now, let's see how a pilot suffering from checkitis will perform. When the motor is cut, he looks down at the fields below him and wonders: "Which field does the inspector prefer that I select? He must have one in mind. Which one is it?" He should be thinking: "Which field offers the best possibilities for a safe landing? Which one is the most practical for me? Which one can I get into without mussing up this airplane?"

At each step he is thinking, "I wonder if this is the way he wants me to do it?" He should be thinking, "I can do it this way. This is the surest and safest way to get down into that field in one piece."

Because of dividing his attention, he fumbles and acts indecisively. How can he act decisively when he is trying to satisfy two goals? He may run into conflict. It may seem to him that the way he knows he can do it may not be the way the inspector wants him to do it. He puts emphasis on unimportant details to make it look good—instead of making it good.

Both checkitis and buck fever cause one to put on his worst performance when he is extremely anxious to do his best: through trying to please the person who is giving him the check ride in the case of checkitis; and through overanxiety to get the job finished in the case of buck fever. In both cases, failure results from not keeping the attention directed to the immediate problem at hand.

Some individuals cannot perform well under pressure because they think of their problem as an overpowering thing, possessing many opportunities for failure, instead of thinking of it in terms of a lot of easy steps, then keeping their attention directed to each step in its turn.

# 16

# The Psychology of Airsickness

Hogan was one of my best instructors. Both Hogan and myself liked to get away from the grind of instructing. So, whenever a cross-country flight developed, we made it a practice to flip a coin to see which one of us would make the flight.

We didn't flip for that flight up into northern Minnesota because Jack Strawn and Hogan were pals, and Strawn, who had just purchased an airplane from us, wanted Hogan to accompany him on the trip. The night before the flight, the two cronies celebrated a bit and were a little the worse for wear the following morning.

Over the wild country of northern Minnesota, Hogan's stomach began to find its contents undesirable and showed some inclination to make a prompt eviction. There was no place to land and Hogan became progressively sicker.

Then it happened! The motor quit. Hogan, a skillful pilot, made a nice landing in what appeared to be an inviting green pasture but turned out to be a bog. The wheels sank deep and the airplane turned over on its back.

After that we didn't flip to decide who was to take the cross-country flights. Hogan didn't want them. He became desperately airsick even on a short cross-country flight, though he could still mill around the airport, instructing for hours at a time, with no uneasiness in his digestive tract. If anything would make a man airsick, why wouldn't these rough rides with students, weaving up and down all over the sky?

Sure, it was all in his head. Hogan knew that as well as I did, but the knowledge wasn't any comfort when he became desperately airsick a few miles out from the airport.

217

One day a psychiatrist, bound for a clinic in a distant city, chartered one of our planes and I flew him. In our conversation at lunch I happened to mention Hogan's trouble. He was greatly interested and told me that, if I would send Hogan to see him, he believed he could help him.

Hogan jumped at the chance. The psychiatrist explained Hogan's trouble to him somewhat as follows: "In flying, you are subject to certain stimuli arising in the labyrinthine canals of the inner ear, which conflict with the stimuli coming in from your eyes. This conflict produces vertigo, which results in nausea. Ordinarily, you do not notice these disturbing stimuli from the labyrinthine canals because you have learned to trust your vision and ignore these conflicting stimuli.

"However, there is such a close relationship between nausea and vertigo that when you are nauseated your attention is directed to the stimuli that cause vertigo and the condition becomes progressively worse. That was your trouble during your flight over the North Woods. You had a hangover of nausea from your overindulgence of the previous night, which caused your attention to be directed to these disturbing stimuli from the labyrinthine canals. Your nausea thus became progressively worse up to the time of your crack-up."

Then he explained the mechanism of these labyrinthine canals to Hogan: "Experimental evidence clearly indicates that airsickness results from vertigo, which is a confused whirling sensation in the head resulting from confusion, in that the sensation of movement which the brain has interpreted from the stimuli coming from the labyrinthine canals does not agree with the interpretation of stimuli coming in from the eyes."

Suppose we examine the structure of the inner ear.

The labyrinths which are stimulated by motion are the utriculus, the sacculus, and the semicircular canals.

The utriculus and the sacculus inform you which way is up and which way is down. They provide clues that indicate the position of the head relative to the pull of gravity.

Little hair cells rise from the floor of these organs. Atop

each hair cell is a tiny bit of lime, sometimes called an earstone. The weight of this earstone causes the hair to bend. The other end of the hair cell connects to nerve fiber, so that the stimuli arising from the bending of this hair are interpreted by the brain to make you aware of the position of your head relative to the pull of gravity.

Some interesting experiments have been conducted with crayfish, in which a tiny iron filing is substituted for the earstone. Then, if a magnet is held over the head of the crayfish, it will promptly turn over onto its back.

It can be seen that centrifugal force causes a misinterpretation of these stimuli, just as the magnet did with the crayfish. Thus, if you lie atop a spinning table, so that you are rotated or swung around in a circle, the centrifugal force to which you are subjected will be difficult to distinguish from the pull of gravity. Such findings do not agree with the stimuli coming in from the eye. That is why centrifugal force may produce nausea.

The semicircular canals, however, produce the worst confusion and are the more common offenders. There are three of these canals. Each one lies in a different one of the three planes of space; each one at right angles to the planes in which the other two canals lie. Each of these semicircular canals is a small, hollow tube filled with a liquid known as endolymph. The tube is curved in the form of a rough, incomplete circle, bulging out into a sort of bulb before completing the circle. Next to the bulb, the canal widens to form the ampulla, from the floor of which tiny hair cells rise or project.

Movements of the head in the plane of one of these canals produce a relative movement between the liquid within the canal and these tiny hairs because of a lag in the movement of the liquid, attributable to its inertia. This motion of the fluid, relative to the hair, causes the hair to bend in the direction of the movement of the fluid, thereby initiating a stimulus which the brain interprets into movement and direction of movement.

When the movement of the head ceases, the liquid

continues to move because of its inertia, and the hair is then bent in a direction opposite to the direction of the preceding movement, with the stimuli arising from this bending again being interpreted as motion in the opposite direction, although your eyes inform you that your head is not moving.

This confusion between the interpretation of the stimuli arising in the labyrinths and the stimuli arising in the eye produces vertigo which in turn causes nausea.

Now if the mind were to ignore one set of these stimuli patterns, there would be no confusion, no vertigo, and no nausea. The brain has learned to accomplish this adaptation to a remarkable degree where approaching and receding motions are concerned, because we are continually involved in such movements and the stimuli arising from the canal which lies in the plane effected by this fore and aft horizontal motion are largely ignored. Where vertical motion is involved, however, we have no such extensive background of experience. Hence we may experience an odd feeling when traveling up and down in an elevator.

It is the inertia upon the starting and stopping of a movement that produces the stimuli in the labyrinthine canals. Because of the circular shape of the canals, the sensations are more noticeable if the motion is of a rotary character, such as is characteristic of the movements of a plane in rough air or a boat in rough water, wherein our movement is in the form of a modified arc.

We can relieve this feeling by lying down, since, in this position, the canal which ordinarily lies in the horizontal plane of movement is stimulated, and the brain is more likely to ignore the stimuli originating in this canal.

We now have one more semicircular canal to consider, the one which lies in the plane that is affected by a sideways movement of the head. As in the case of the back-and-forth movement, we have a considerable fund of experience in this sideways movement and it does not disturb us overly much except where the rotation is complete. We have little experience with continuous rotation since our head is not mounted so that it normally revolves in a complete 360-degree circle.

However, there is a reflex movement of the eyeball which helps us adjust to rotations. You can demonstrate this by placing an individual in a whirling chair. Spin him around about ten times in twenty seconds; then stop the rotation and have him look at a spot directly in front of himself, and watch his eyes. If you have rotated him to the right, you will notice that while looking straight ahead, his eyes move slowly to the left and then jerk back to center again. They will continue to do this for fifteen or twenty seconds, until the fluid in the labyrinthine canals settles down a bit from the inertia generated by the rotation. If you rotate him to the left, the action will be reversed. That is, his eyes will swing slowly to the right and then jerk back to center again.

Perhaps you have watched a ballet dancer spin around on the polished ballroom floor or the stage. You have noticed that she quickly jerks her head in a series of sudden movements as she spins. You will observe that there is a similarity in the movement of her head and in the movements of the eyeballs described in the experiment. She has learned that, by keeping her eyes fixed on a definite point as she turns, she can avoid becoming dizzy and losing her balance. Of course, since she is turning, it is impossible to keep the eyes focused on one point continually; so, as this point gets near the edge of her range of vision, she quickly swings her head to a new point.

This is one reason why the pilot of an airplane is less likely to become airsick than is a passenger. When flying, the pilot unconsciously accomplishes in a less exaggerated manner what the dancer accomplishes by the violent jerks of her head as she spins around. Instead of allowing his vision to swing with the motion of the airplane, the pilot focuses it on some feature that he observes in connection with his flying and quickly switches his vision from point to point as he switches his attention from one detail to another. The focal point of his vision does not swing with the motion of the airplane.

The passenger who is sitting relaxed in his seat, looking at nothing in particular, may not adapt to the motion of the airplane so well because he does not have to focus his vision on definite points and he may allow his field of vision to rotate with the airplane.

Of course, the pilot is so busy that his attention is directed to his duties instead of searching for signs of oncoming nausea.

Then, too, one is less likely to become airsick when looking ahead at some distant point on the horizon. If you ride the airlines very much, you may have observed that the hostess often disappears through the door to the pilot's compartment, not to reappear again for some ten or fifteen minutes. Hostesses have confided to me that they do not go forward to carry on a little romancing with the pilots, nor for an important conference, but to seek relief when they find themselves becoming nauseated, for when they stand in the pilot's compartment and look straight ahead at the horizon, they find the nausea leaving them.

All motion would produce nausea, because of these conflicting stimuli from the labyrinthine canals, if we did not learn to adapt ourselves to these confusing stimuli.

When a man takes up flying, he is subjected to these confusing stimuli in planes of motion to which he has not learned to adapt himself so well. It takes a little time, but he eventually learns to adapt to these new motions, provided he encounters these conditions in easy stages. However, if his first experience in flying involves air so rough that he cannot adjust to it, he becomes airsick, and he may have difficulty in learning to adjust to the condition.

The wise flying instructor starts the student out in smooth air and avoids maneuvers that may nauseate him. Any time he observes any discomfort upon the part of the student he should land before the student becomes airsick. The wise instructor knows that one may keep on flying if he is frightened a little, for mild fear can even prove pleasingly stimulating, but there is nothing stimulating about airsickness, and the student who experiences airsickness is likely to give up flying.

There seems to be some relation between this tendency to become airsick and pilot proficiency. Army records show that 52 per cent of the pilots who have suffered from airsickness have later washed out before completing the course of training. This figure is probably much higher in civilian flying, since the Air Force endeavors to eliminate individuals sensitive to airsickness, by means of careful tests made while selecting candidates for flight training.

Air Force records also show that students who develop a tendency to become airsick became airsick at some time during their first few lessons. An intelligent instructor, by using proper care in breaking a student into rough air and violent maneuvers, can greatly reduce the number of problem students and at the same time lose fewer students who quit because they get airsick. Such students seldom tell their instructor why they quit. They just drift away from the flying field.

Of course, in some individuals the labyrinthine passages have been destroyed by disease or are less sensitive than normal, and we find other persons in whom these passages are extremely sensitive.

"Now in your case, Mr. Hogan," said the psychiatrist, "you had flown for a long time and were well adjusted to these confusing stimuli, until some experience put you back to where you can no longer adjust to them.

"Fortunately, in your case, we know just what that experience was. At the time you crashed, there was no landing field available where you could land and seek relief from your nausea. Now you have come to look upon every crosscountry flight as such a condition, unconsciously overlooking the fact that you can land if you wish. This causes you to be afraid that you will become airsick, and, unconsciously, you direct your attention to trying to discover the first symptoms of oncoming nausea. Hence, you are aware of every disturbing movement of the airplane, and these disturbing stimuli soon make you sick.

"When you have a student up, flying around the airport,

you are not afraid of this situation, because you know you can go in and land any time you want to. You do not direct your attention to trying to detect oncoming symptoms of nausea, and you are not so aware of these disturbing stimuli from the labyrinthine canals.

"Here is what I want you to do. Take an airplane out for a cross-country flight tomorrow. You have flat country all around you here, so that you can land almost anywhere. Do just that. At the first moment you find yourself becoming nauseated, go down and land, and stay on the ground until you feel O.K., and then take off again. Repeat this as often as you feel nauseated, even if you have to make a hundred landings before you complete the flight. As a matter of fact, I doubt if you have to make more than one or two landings, and it would not surprise me if you did not have to make a single landing. Once you have a solution of this problem available, you will quit looking for symptoms of nausea and will again adjust as you formerly learned to do, to these confusing stimuli from the labyrinthine passages."

It worked with Hogan, and I found I had gypped myself out of a lot of cross-country flights by sending him to the psychiatrist.

It is interesting to point out that, although this confusion ordinarily comes from the misleading stimuli arising in the labyrinthine passages, it can be the other way around; it can come from confusing stimuli arising in the eyes. This is what happens when, sitting in one train, you observe another train pulling out of the railroad station, where only a foot or so separates you from the moving train, blotting out all view of any other objects for comparison; all you can see is the moving car from your view from the window.

Your eyes fool you. It seems as though you are moving and the other train is standing still. Since you are not actually moving, you know that the labyrinthine passages are not being stimulated. It is thus obvious that the condition is produced by misinterpretation of the stimuli from the eyes. The same phenomenon may be observed in other visual illusions wherein you have the feeling of motion when you actually are not moving.

We maintain our equilibrium automatically, through reflexes whose centers lie in the medulla oblongata of the hind brain. It is rather significant that the nerve fibers from the sacculus, the utriculus, and the semicircular canals lead to the medulla.

The reflex center for vomiting is also located in the medulla. This has been demonstrated in animals by cutting the spinal cord across just below the medulla, whereupon it has been observed that vomiting is abolished. No effect on vomiting is produced by a cross section above the medulla.

There are drugs that decrease the sensitiveness of the labyrinthine passages but they also have side effects that would make their use by a pilot inadvisable. The same is true of sedatives that furnish some relief through decreasing all sensations.

Care in avoiding the overloading of the stomach, particularly with heavy starches or fats, may help. Well-cooked, lean meat seems to agree with the airsick passenger as well as anything. Too much liquid may slosh around in the stomach, adding to your discomfort. Foods that produce gas, such as beans, cabbage and others, also may be upsetting. Disagreeable odors, such as oil fumes or exhaust gases, may also aggravate airsickness.

However, the real cure lies in adjusting to these confusing stimuli from the labyrinthine canals. We cannot succeed in doing this when we direct our attention to them as we do when we are afraid of becoming airsick. We are more likely to succeed when our attention is directed to some duty, as is the case with the pilot.

Once one has a distressing case of airsickness, he may be unable to adjust to these confusing stimuli, because he cannot keep his mind off them; he continually directs his attention to them. He keeps checking to see if he can recognize any of these distressing stimuli, and when he looks for them he is almost sure to find them.

Herein we find an almost exact parallel to the lack of confidence that is produced by failure. The best way to build confidence is to avoid failure, and the best way to prevent airsickness is to avoid becoming airsick in the first place. Much of the responsibility for this lies with flying instructors.

# 17

# The Psychology of Instrument Flying

"The local girls are friendly and there is plenty of whiskey."

After this glowing tribute to the social advantages of the Midwestern city which adjoined the air base, the colonel made it clear that we would have little opportunity to avail ourselves of these tempting pleasures. Our schedule called for a day of highly concentrated activity, starting at 6:30 in the morning when we turned out for calisthenics, progressing from one activity to another, with an occasional ten-minute break, and from thirty to sixty minutes out for meals, until 9:30 at night. This schedule covered seven days of the week.

I doubt if Colonel Simon Legree could distinguish between an oven thermometer and a turn-and-bank-indicator, but he was the commanding officer of the first Army Gauge School that I flunked.

He possessed the priceless, hard-boiled qualities of the "Old School" army officer, and these sterling qualities were not seriously diluted with any of the congenialities usually a part of a human being.

He concluded his fireside chat with the warning that he intended to keep us busy every minute and that his long list of rules would be strictly enforced. Offenders would be confined to their quarters and barred from the PX. This latter penalty may seem like an odd disciplinary measure to one who doesn't understand that a trip to the PX for a package of cigarettes was the highest form of recreation offered at this post.

With students in a rebellious mood, and with their mental activity slowed and dulled by the long, tiring hours of concentration, unrelieved by any recreation other than the old army stand-by—calisthenics by the "one-two"—is it any wonder that there was a high percentage of students who failed to qualify?

Major Patterson, who knew instrument flying—and men— organized an instrument school very differently when he was faced with the problem of training that first group of pilots who were sent to Africa from the post where the major was stationed. This school was one of those priority deals, and the major had less than half the time that was needed to train this group of fliers properly.

Scotty, a short, red-headed, cotton-duster from Arkansas, told me about Major Patterson and his instrument school.

"Hell!" said Scotty, "the major acts more like a human being than an army officer. He tells us to relax and let him do the worrying. He assures us that we are all going to complete the course. Right off the bat, he said, 'You won't be tied to a rigid schedule. If you have trouble at some point with some phase of the training, we will just devote a little more time until you get it. We are going to take it easy and you won't be hurried. You will be excused from calisthenics, drill, and all other non-essential, routine activities.' "

That's how a smart man, who knew instrument flying from A to Z, tackled this problem where he was working against time. It paid off. He had the good will and the cooperation of his students. Every minute that they flew they were right on the ball, with their mental processes working at top speed. He instilled confidence in them right from the very beginning. The major turned out a group of qualified instrument pilots in record time.

If doctor's degrees were issued to pilots, they would undoubtedly be given to those who have earned their instrument cards.

To become a capable instrument pilot, the flyer must learn to do three things exceedingly well:

1. He must learn to fly with precision.

2. He must learn to trust the accuracy of the instruments that substitute for visual reference. (He can never hope to do this unless he ignores the stimuli arising in his labyrinthine and somatic receptors.)

3. He must learn the various procedures, let-down problems, orientation problems, and beam bracketing so thoroughly that he does not lose sight of the problem as a whole while keeping his attention on the step at hand. This means that he must be able to work these problems in a step-by-step procedure, keeping himself oriented to the relation between the step he is performing and the entire problem without taking his attention away from each step as he performs it.

Aside from its utilitarian value, the course of training should improve the efficiency of any pilot because this ability to keep ourselves oriented to the problem as a whole without taking our attention away from the step at hand enters into the solution of any problem of action that must be broken down into easy steps and then solved a step at a time. In instrument flying one must develop this ability to a high degree, for failure at any step cannot be tolerated.

Many instrument instructors seem to believe that the most important thing about the entire course is to demonstrate to the student in the very beginning that he is in for a rough time. It is highly unfortunate that many instructors feel that there is some intrinsic advantage in continually demonstrating the difficulties to a student.

Through a study of conditioning we know that we learn by building upon what we already know, through association. Where an instructor fails to take students through an instrument course in easy steps, he is likely to be rewarded by a high percentage of failures.

Many students have not mastered precision flying when they begin their instrument training. It is nearly hopeless to proceed with training under the hood before the student has demonstrated the ability to fly by the instruments with some degree of precision.

One must practice a long time under the hood before he learns how to level off smoothly by the use of the instruments, especially if he is restricted to the use of the airspeed indicator, rate-of-climb indicator, and altimeter. If he is first allowed to practice this leveling off by the use of instruments without the hood so that he may compare the procedure with his normal contact procedure, he will learn quickly.

The instructor can force the student to use the instruments more and visual contacts less by insisting that he stay within such precise limits that he must continually refer to the instruments to stay within these limits. This requirement not only teaches the student to use the instruments but to rely upon them as well. Simultaneously, he develops the precision that is so essential to instrument flight.

The customary practice of placing the student under the hood before he has learned to use the instruments makes it exceedingly difficult for him to ignore his somatic and labyrinthine sensations. As he is deprived of the benefits of his sense of vision, he makes use of the labyrinthine and somatic senses which as we know are not to be relied upon.

If he is first trained to use the instruments before he is placed under the hood, he is not deprived of his sense of vision—he merely switches it from points outside the cockpit to the instruments.

Let-down problems, orientation problems, and beam bracketing also are learned with greater ease where the student is allowed to practice them a few times without the hood. Of course, many students feel that this is kindergarten stuff and rebel against such easy steps. These are often the students who fail.

Where the instructor attempts to develop precision at the same time that the student is learning procedure, the problem is interrupted frequently because the student strays too far away from the limits. I have known of cases where, as a result of such interruption, a student received practically all of his training on the first half of a problem—never reaching the last half because of these interruptions. This is an ideal method for breaking down a student's confidence. He learns to fail right in the middle of every problem.

The student should be compelled to develop sufficient precision so that he may be allowed to muddle through every problem he starts. Interrupting a problem before completion is justified only when the student has failed at some step in the procedure. Even then it is better to let him muddle through if possible. If he gets lost, let him orient himself and start over again. That is what he will have to do when he is actually flying on instruments. During the course of training is an ideal time to learn such procedures.

If the instructor is alert and watchful, he can detect the student's weak points from the manner in which he muddles through a problem in the early stages. Then, after the problem has been completed, the instructor can drill the student on these weak points. Once the problem has started, however, it should not be interrupted—the student should be allowed to work to its final conclusion just as he would do in actual instrument weather.

Some instructors talk too much. They don't give the student time to discover and correct his own mistakes but keep up such a continual line of chatter that the student is confused.

Where the problem must be continually interrupted, it is an indication that the student is not ready to begin work on the problem. This does not mean that the instructor should not keep giving the student a gentle nudge when he lets his eyes remain on one instrument too long and begins to edge away from the limits established for precision.

When the Link trainer is available, it can be used to advantage for learning procedures, and thus costly time in the air can be saved. Here again many instructors seem to believe that there is some intrinsic advantage in making it difficult for the student to learn. All the student learns from the use of the trainer is procedures, and on procedures the emphasis should be placed in Link training.

The Link trainer does not fly exactly like an airplane. The peculiar skill essential to mastering the trainer serves little useful purpose; hence there is no point in adjusting the trainer to so sensitive a point that the student cannot master his procedures.

Many instructors start the student on beam bracketing with only the rudder released so that the student is not handicapped by the necessity for using ailerons and elevator. This method of instruction is also practical when drilling on orientation procedures. Once the procedures have been learned, the problem can be made more difficult by releasing the ailerons and elevator, giving the student more to do.

As in the airplane it is well to let the student complete the problem once he has started it.

When the student has mastered all his procedures, rough air and icing conditions may be simulated to make the problem more difficult. The student learns with greater ease if he is taken along in a step-by-step procedure, difficulties being added as the student develops to the point where he can meet them successfully.

It is the duty of an instrument instructor to "temper the burden to the back of the ass," as the proverb says. The most common mistake in instrument training is to surround the student continually with so many difficulties that he fails again and again. Instead of teaching him to fly on instruments, the instructor is conditioning him to fail.

Because of the mass of detail, the precision, and the timing required, the instrument pilot must be alert, with his mental processes working with smooth rapidity. Confidence produces such a mental state, and a lack of confidence destroys it. Hence confidence is essential to the capable instrument pilot. Where a course of instruction in instrument flying fails to instill confidence in the student, it is of questionable value.

# 18

# The Temperament of the Pilot

As the airliner passed over South Bend, Indiana, the pilot noticed that the indicator showed no oil pressure for the left outboard motor. He promptly shut down the motor, feathered its propeller, and proceeded to Chicago on one engine. He radioed ahead advising Chicago of his difficulty, and when he reached the airport he found all other traffic halted. He was immediately given his clearance to land.

Now a twin-engine airplane such as this pilot was flying can maintain flight on one engine until the undercarriage is lowered for the landing. After that the added resistance of the landing gear makes it impossible to maintain altitude on a single engine.

At the time there was such a heavy wind blowing that, in effect, the approach leg was lengthened. The airplane lost altitude rapidly and it crashed through a house that lay in its path.

During their course of training on multi-engine aircraft, pilots are taught to shut down an engine and feather the propeller when the oil pressure has been lost. However, a cautious pilot would certainly start the motor again to have it available in case of emergency before he began his final approach to the runway.

The C.A.A. in this case terminated the pilot's rating. It was strongly justified in so doing because this pilot lacked a component of temperament that fosters old age—the desire to stay alive.

In many individuals this desire to stay alive seems to transfer itself to foolish pride or to various motivations of an aggressive character.

233

Pilots have a trite proverb:

"There are old pilots and there are bold pilots but there are no old bold pilots."

I remember one time when a salesman in his sales talk said to a prospect for an airplane flight, "What are you worrying about? Don't you know you won't die till your time comes?"

"I know," replied the prospective passenger, "but I am afraid the pilot's time may come when I am riding with him."

You and I feel as though we are riding with a madman when we ride with a pilot who does not make a deliberate attempt to stay alive.

I dislike to speak of types because each one of us is a very special type the like of which the world has never before seen. Yet it is somewhat difficult to identify the trait we seek.

If we identify these adaptive responses that so often place us within the shadow of death by labeling them under the general head of boldness, then the opposite pole would be timidity—boldness vs. timidity.

Suppose we examine further this trait of scorning the safe and easy way of doing things.

"Can you see the runway?"

I was on final approach to the runway at Albuquerque, New Mexico. The tower was asking the question. The heavy wind that was blowing at the time was sweeping clouds of dust and sand into the air. At times the runway appeared indistinct.

I landed without difficulty and reported to Operations to close my flight plan. There I learned that another B-24 was approaching the airport with one of the outboard motors dead. I thought to myself, "This wind is a break for him— not much likelihood of his overshooting."

I watched the bomber as it approached for the landing. The pilot was apparently having difficulties. It seemed to require a terrific effort for him to hold up the wing with the dead engine, and he was drifting off his flight path. He ended up by landing slightly cross-wind and missing the runway entirely.

On the first bounce the undercarriage was so badly

damaged that it dangled limply like a broken limb. At the next contact with the ground the fuselage sheared in two just behind the flight deck. The airplane came to rest in a crumpled heap.

There was an easy method for making this approach that would have made such a disaster unlikely. On his final approach, the pilot could have throttled back his other outboard motor, thus eliminating the uneven yaw and making it easier to control the airplane. Using his two inboard motors would have reduced the four-engine bomber to a twin-engine airplane, and he would have had all the power he needed for his final approach. Instead he tried to do it the hard way—and death took its toll.

During training, a multi-engine pilot is required to make landings with various simulated conditions of power failure as a means to develop the skill he needs. In an emergency, common-sense should impel him to adopt the easiest possible manner of approach, one that requires the least skill and hence offers the least possibility for failure.

Perhaps the trait we are seeking could be labeled: common-sense vs. foolish pride

Two boys approach a stream. One boy tries to leap across it and lands in the water. The other boy goes out of his way a few steps and crosses over a bridge.

Two men come to a fork in the road. The only information available to them is that either of the two highways open to their selection will take them to their destination. One highway is smoothly paved; the other is rough and rocky. Common-sense impels one man to take the smooth highway, whereas some damn-fool feeling that there is something intrinsically heroic about doing things the hard way impels the other man to take the rough road.

Two students are learning to fly. One continually lashes the control stick all around the cockpit with numerous needless motions. The other student makes only the motions necessary to pick up a low wing or to bring the airplane back on course. In the second case, the emotions of the student flowed smoothly.

We see a hint that the trait we are seeking may involve:
reserve and placidity vs. aggressiveness

We all come into the world with a drive for self-preservation. We retreat from those things that can injure or destroy us. Why do we depart from this pattern of behavior?

The culture to which we are subjected places a high value upon courage, determination, and similar virtues. Therein arises a conflict between self-preservation and the approval of the group to which we belong. We seek to develop responses that will satisfy both, but we may lean too far in our efforts to gain the approval of our group.

For instance: If a man is drowning, the group admires one who, at the risk of losing his own life, will dive into the water and tow the drowning man to safety. But if you or I cannot swim a stroke, is there any point in either of us diving into the water to lose his own life with no possible chance of aiding the drowning man?

The group admires a person who will make personal sacrifices to aid others. A mother scrimps, saves, and works so hard to send her two sons through college that she ruins her own health and dies before either boy has completed his education. Has she placed either of those boys in a better position to meet life by throwing away her own? If we are unsympathetic, we may even suspect that it was the approval of the group to which she belonged rather than the welfare of her sons that prompted her sacrifices.

You and I are influenced by a culture that places an overwhelming emphasis upon aggressiveness. The man who does things is greatly admired, and his motivation for doing them is seldom questioned. Is it to be wondered that some of us go through life in a continual flurry of action that doesn't seem to accomplish much—in fact, often defeats the ver^ purpose of action? Is it any wonder that some people seem to act for the love of action rather than from a desire to accomplish something worthwhile?

When we make a nice compromise between self-preservation and gaining the approval of the group to which we belong, when we put first things first and second things second, we are said to be endowed with common-sense, and fortunately there is a growing tendency for our culture to approve of common-sense. On this premise we will label the trait that we are seeking common-sense, although it might be more properly labeled an uncommonly good sense of values.

Common-sense seems to involve a number of compromises, as can be seen by the following examples.

timidity vs. boldness

reserve and placidity vs. aggressiveness

things important to survival vs. public opinion

A philosophy of life is an aid to developing common-sense since it provides us with a measuring stick with which to judge values.

My own philosophy of life can be reduced to exceedingly simple terms: Anything that hurts any human being (and this includes myself) is wrong. Anything that aids or brings pleasure to any human being (and this also includes myself) is right. That is my simple formula for determining the difference between sin and virtue and the magnitude of each.

A philosophy of life aids us to get set to make the desired response. When we get set to make a certain response, we are likely to make that response.

For example: You have watched a cat poised alertly before a hole in the baseboard waiting for a mouse to make its appearance, and you know that the instant the mouse pokes its head out the cat will pounce. You have watched the same cat, with its back arched and its tail alertly inflated, eyeing the dog it is facing, and you know that at the first favorable opportunity the cat will scamper across the lawn and up a tree.

In like manner a philosophy of life serves as a sort of master plan that gets us set to make the desired responses in the varying situations that we encounter.

The unique responses that we characteristically make to various patterns of stimuli are evoked by the stimuli that have acted upon us. We are molded by the stimuli that bombard us from within and from without. We might think of ourselves as plastic material, each of us a different kind of plastic—each of us made of a material possessing its own unique qualities.

We are exceedingly plastic at birth, and a definite pattern of adaptations that we call temperament is quickly developed. As we grow older, we continually become less plastic—we become set in our ways.

Since we are very plastic early in life, parents and teachers try to control our early environment. We are acted upon by stimuli in such a manner as to mold our personality along lines which our parents and teachers believe will result in a personality that will enable us to adjust to life in a satisfactory manner.

Psychologists are justified in placing great emphasis upon the importance of the early years of life when the child is exceedingly plastic. During these years the child gets set for life. But you and I should never infer that this emphasis upon the early environment implies that we, ourselves, being the product of heredity plus environment, can do nothing further about it.

You and I possess a nervous system that enables us to understand how we are molded by the stimuli that act upon us. We can also understand why we possess the unique patterns of response that we call our personality. We can understand how our motivations have developed from the stimuli to which we have been exposed. Understanding these things, we can plan to expose ourselves to favorable stimuli so far as possible and to react favorably, in so far as we can, to the stimuli we may encounter.

This is the reason that we study psychology—to attain an understanding that enables us to mold our own personality further, that enables us to take over where our parents and teachers left off. Psychology is a significant, correlated organization of the facts of human behavior and the facts that we possess concerning the construction and operation of the nervous system.

To apply psychology, we use indirect methods to attain our ends. Knowing the cause points to a way for getting the desired effect. In most cases patience is required, since we are living organisms that develop through growth, and our adaptive responses involve a progress of growth.

It is true that in adult life we are dealing with a material that has lost much of its plasticity, but it can still be molded.

How?

1. By developing a philosophy of life—by making plans upon which we get set to act. We have stressed the reversibility of mental phenomena. According to the James-Lang theory:

We act > as < we feel

Hence we can develop proper motivations by doing the things those motivations would cause us to do.

2. We do the desired things by planning our responses beforehand when we are not swayed by the emotion that the situation provokes. (This plan becomes a new motivation in itself.) Then we are set to make the desired response when we encounter the situation, just as the cat poised before the hole in the baseboard was set to pounce upon the luckless mouse.

3. Through selection of a favorable environment we can place ourselves in locations and in situations where we are most likely to be acted upon by stimuli that will encourage the desired response and promote the desired motivations.

If an alcoholic associates with other alcoholics, he is likely to find himself before a long bar with his foot on a brass rail, and he will probably encounter stimuli that will encourage him to stow away a few "boilermakers" and other potent libations.

If he associates with the members of his local church or with members of Alcoholics Anonymous, he is less likely to be acted upon by stimuli that will cause him to "fall off the wagon," and eventually his motivations may undergo a change.

If a pilot associates with reckless daredevils, he is likely to find himself motivated toward reckless behavior. If he associates with safe and sane pilots who have the welfare of flying at heart and who prize their own necks highly, he is likely to find himself developing common-sense motivations.

The pilot whose motivations are built upon a common-sense attitude gives himself every break. He doesn't show off. He makes a deliberate attempt to stay alive by avoiding situations that demand all the skill he possesses—and possibly a bit more. He takes the smooth, easy road that demands the least skill and effort when that smooth, easy road leads safely to effective action.

# 19
# The Personality of the Pilot

Fiction writers delight in characterizing the airplane pilot as a happy-go-lucky, don't-give-a-damn sort of fellow. Such carefree personalities flit through the pages of fiction in reckless fashion, continually caught with their necks out, just as their thoughtless prototypes do in real life. Their reckless behavior frequently brings them to the brink of disaster, just as such behavior can be expected to endanger the careless pilot on the flying field and in the air.

The writer of fiction seeks to bring his hero within a split-second of eternity to dangle in suspense until in a dramatic climax he is rescued with a few strokes of the pen. A real flesh-and-blood pilot is more likely to lose his life or spill considerable blood in such intriguing circumstances.

You and I have motivations that impel us to take direct action in seeking pleasure and avoiding pain and discomfort. We have other motivations that take the future into consideration, for we value pleasure and freedom from discomfort in the future as much as or more than we value them at the moment. Our primitive motivations and our motivations for security often meet in head-on conflict.

Freud with his fancy for symbolism liked to think of these conflicting emotions as individuals fighting for dominance within us. He coined the symbol "id" to represent the primitive impulses inherent in all of us. He used the word "ego" to represent self, the conscious mind with its drive for self-expression. He used the term "super-ego" to represent what you and I call conscience, which he thought of as a sort of "censor" of the individual in his personal and in his social adaptations.

When I was a boy on the farm, we had a bull named Julius. Sometimes a neighbor would bring a bovine admirer to call on Julius. He would be lying in a sunny corner of his domicile, thoughtfully munching a wisp of hay, apparently half asleep.

Suddenly his sleepy eyes would open wide and he would scramble to his feet emitting a throaty bellow of welcome, and someone would shout, "Julius Sees'er!"

Julius seemed to possess a strong "ego" and he was such a hand for direct action that I am sure his personality included a powerfully developed "id." So far as we were ever able to discover, Julius did not possess a "super-ego" to censor either his "id" or his "ego."

Julius was an excellent performer in his own way. His effective action may be traced to a remarkable freedom from mental conflict.

This in no way implies that you and I should envy Julius for his happy-go-lucky, don't-give-a-damn personality. We possess nervous systems with superior powers of integration; we can make a choice and thereby settle our conflicts. Such effort is a small price to pay for our ability to plan for the future. You and I can adapt to circumstances that would mean the end of green pastures for Julius.

Our desire for security in the physical world conflicts with the motivations that would displease our fellows or in any way threaten our future happiness. Our desire for security in the spiritual world conflicts with the motivations that would displease our God.

The motivations involved are nearly identical, since we conceive of acts that injure or displease our fellows as being contrary to God's wishes. Of course, we may believe that we can conceal our acts and our motivations from our fellows, but we have a feeling that God knows all, so the desire to please God imposes a more rigid censorship than does the desire to please our fellows.

In short—conscience is that still, small voice that bids us take the future into consideration, the sum total of our motivations for security.

Since what we do in the present affects our future, a nagging conscience may impair our ability to adjust satisfactorily either for the present or for the future. At times we are wise to investigate our motivations for security and the motivations with which they conflict and make sure that a threat to our future does actually exist; also we should make sure that we censor only those actions that would displease our fellows or our God.

For instance: We have learned that, if we mingle with clean, well-dressed people in clean, fastidious surroundings, we must also be clean and properly attired, else we may offend these people. If we offend them, they are likely to take punitive action; they may actually kick us out or they may scorn or dislike us because of our uncouth behavior.

However, people ordinarily do not take offense at acts that are essential to our survival or to our job, even though under other circumstances these same acts might prove offensive.

We must learn to consider not our acts alone, but the circumstances that may justify them as well.

For example: If Harry Hawkins enters a fastidious Country Club where men in tails and ladies in evening gowns are dancing, and if Harry is wearing a pair of grimy overalls soaked with perspiration and his hands and face are spotted with grease and grime, he will naturally give offense.

Suppose, however, that Harry Hawkins happens to be the plumber who has been called in to repair the plumbing in the clubhouse? Certainly no one expects Harry to bathe, shave, and don a tuxedo before coming on the job. Sensible people think nonetheless of him because of his grimy overalls. But if, because of the similarity of the two situations, Harry applies the same rigid rules of censorship to the second situation that he applies to the first situation, he feels uncomfortable. He may hurry to get out of this unpleasant situation with little attention directed to his work and may do a slipshod bit of plumbing.

Foolish? Certainly it's foolish, but how often do you and I

feel uncomfortable when a proper adaptive response is transferred to another situation where it does not fit at all despite the similarity of the two situations.

The solution does not lie in refusing to value security. It lies in learning to analyze the two similar situations to discover why the response for number one should not be used for number two. If we can discover no valid reason for the feeling of anxiety or guilt in the second situation, we can condition ourselves to choose the proper course of action and stick to it with no further embarrassment.

Sometimes there is a very valid reason for our anxiety.

Oscar is enjoying the thrill of flying a hundred feet above the tree tops but he does not feel comfortable. Forebodings of impending disaster nag him with a depressing insistence. If Oscar will analyze the situation, he will discover that there is a well-founded reason for his feeling of guilt, since he will be in a tough spot if his motor suddenly quits. Recognizing that there is a valid reason for his anxiety, he can remove the threat to his security by climbing to a safe altitude.

Now for a case where anxiety is not justified.

Early in his flying career, Gerald suffered the misfortune of a crack-up while attempting to make a forced landing far from a friendly airport. He has never forgotten how helpless he felt when the motor failed him that day. Now he is troubled with grim forebodings whenever he gets out of sight of an airport. He dreads making a cross-country flight. Suppose he analyzes this feeling. He recognizes at once that this feeling of insecurity has been transferred from that ill-fated, cross-country flight to all cross-country flights.

Yet now it is a different situation. At that time he was an unskilled pilot incompetent to make a forced landing. Since then he has practiced forced landings until he never misses. Any level field is a potential airport. Certainly there is no need for feeling that his fate lies in the hands of Providence once he leaves an airport until he arrives at his destination.

Suppose we use an analogy wherein you are the president

of a large corporation and you have a public relations attorney whose job is to caution you against those actions that might bring punitive measures in the form of a lawsuit against the corporation. The public relations attorney will represent your conscience.

This public relations attorney nags you about impending lawsuits to the point where you are afraid of doing anything at all and you discover that the corporation can no longer develop business in an aggressive manner.

First you should check to make sure that you have not been in the habit of acting before consulting your attorney. Then you should have him sit in on all your planning conferences so that a safe procedure may be developed in the first place. With your plans cleared by him before being put into action, there will be little likelihood of his troubling you further about the matter.

In like manner, isn't it wise to consider the results of our actions before we act? Isn't it wise to plan our actions so that they will not threaten our security and so that we can act with a clear conscience?

Assume, however, that you have acted without consultation, and your public relations attorney is warning you of an impending lawsuit. How about a conference with your attorney? You won't chase around in circles but will analyze the situation and make your plans.

1.  Your first question will be, "Is there something I can do about it? Can I make some settlement that will remove this threat to my security?"

2.  If the answer is yes, you will ask, "Do I want to do something about it?" and finally, "Am I going to do something about it?"

3.  If you answer yes to all those questions, you will make plans to do something, put the plans into action, and that will end the matter—no more nagging from your attorney.

4.  If you answer no anywhere along the line, then you must be prepared to fight the case or to pay the penalty. You

will plan accordingly and that too should end the matter. A decision is reached, and you will instruct your attorney to regard the incident as closed.

A conscience is necessary for constructive action. We must have it to safeguard our security, and it is not likely to handicap us if we think and plan in a decisive manner. Worrying is unorganized, indecisive thinking wherein we tear the situation apart and finger the pieces but fail to put them together again in logical order.

Some people substitute fatalism for logical, decisive thinking. The fatalist has such a feeling of inferiority, inadequacy, and incompetence that he uses this sedative to soothe his conscience, disclaiming all responsibility for his behavior. He says, "If it is going to happen, it will happen; there is nothing I can do about it." Then, with a careless shrug of his shoulders, he adds, "It's just fate."

Larry Soames was a fatalist. He never checked his motor. He never studied the weather sequences. He never planned a flight and usually departed without even a map. He ignored traffic as he taxied out to the last half of the runway for his take-off. Blasting the motor open wide, he would chaundelle up into the sky. He flew low and often slowly.

I told him, "Larry, you are sticking your neck out pretty far. Low flying is especially dangerous in your case since you are not so hot on forced landings."

He laughed. "That's just it; if my motor conks out I know I'll crack up anyway so I fly low to avoid all the suspense."

Larry's flying was soon over with—permanently.

Careful planning fosters the development of a stable personality that enables us to stick to our decisions. But the personality of the airplane pilot should be flexible as well as stable. The manner in which the professional pilot uses his flight plan provides an excellent example of a desirable balance of stability with flexibility.

The professional pilot makes a flight plan with exacting care before he starts on a cross-country trip. He has his estimated time of arrival (E.T.A.) , together with his headings, his altitude, and his air speed, set down for each check point.

Arriving at his first check point, he checks the time as he passes over and compares it with the E.T.A. on his flight plan.

Suppose it doesn't check? Suppose he has missed his E.T.A. by a few minutes? Suppose he notices that he is a little off course? Does he chuck his flight plan out the window, as you and I sometimes abandon our decisions?

No, indeed! Instead he adjusts to the new situation by changing his air speed and, if necessary, his headings to meet the changes. He understands that the direction and the velocity of the wind are subject to change. He knows that the temperature may either rise or fall and that the atmospheric pressure may vary. He simply recognizes the situation and adjusts his flight plan to meet these changes as he encounters them.

This is a fair example of flexible stability. We make our plans and then as we follow them to our goals we maintain contact with reality by observing the changes in the situation and adjusting to those changes as we meet them.

It is seldom necessary to abandon our plans completely when we encounter a change in the situation. Instead, we can adjust to meet such a change and continue toward our goal. The wise planner includes the possibility of change as he makes his plans.

If we are reluctant to recognize and adjust to changing circumstances, we have cause for worry. We are like the boy who wrote down Chicago as the capital of Illinois on his geography examination and then prayed, "Oh God! Please make Chicago the capital of Illinois."

We probe for a miracle or some lucky break instead of recognizing the inevitable and accepting and adjusting to it. We are like a pilot who, when lost, darts first this way and then that, and finally ends up circling, in the forlorn hope that he may sight some familiar landmark, when he should be working out some logical orientation procedure.

If we fail to make careful plans and if we fail to stick to our plans, adjusting those plans to changing circumstances, we may be tempted to accept fatalistic platitudes designed to ease a troubled conscience.

To live for the moment alone, with no thought of the future, refusing to make use of our past, adjusting to life like some dumb animal—all this as a panacea to escape worry —is a mighty poor substitute for careful planning and the willingness to adjust our plans to the changing situation.

# 20

# The Key to Power

You and I want to be effective. We want to be successful. Through the ages various philosophers have sought for some magical key to power that would bring success to those who held it.

Oriental mysticism has attracted some who search for a magic formula for the power and strength to live successfully. Men journey to the high mountains of Tibet to sit at the feet of the Lama high priests. When they return, these men proclaim that they have learned the great secret.

The Rosicrucians declare that they possess a secret method for the mastery of life.

Out in Moscow, Idaho, Dr. Robinson says, "I talked with God," and implies that God revealed these great mysteries of life to him. And I gather that, for a nominal fee, he will pass on some of this vital information to you and me.

We don't have to travel, however, around the world or delve deep into intricate philosophies to discover this key to effective action. A trip through any of our great industrial institutions should make this secret clear to us. It is so absolutely simple, so adaptable to all of our difficult problems, that we are likely to scorn it, and even more likely to fail to understand how we may use it.

American manufacturing methods are being copied all over the world because they are effective. Let's see what makes them so effective.

1. A manufacturing problem is broken down into steps. Each step is so simple that any capable workman can master it and perform it to perfection.

2. Each workman is given a specific job to do. He does not have to worry about a million different problems; all he has to accomplish is this one specific task. He can give it his full

attention and do it well.

Because of this specialization, intricate products can be manufactured, which would be exceedingly difficult, if not impossible, to make by hand, and they can be produced at a fraction of the cost.

By a similar process, you and I can break our difficult problems down into steps so easy that we can master each step, and thus do things which seem extremely difficult, if not impossible. We can do these difficult things with ease, and whittle our production costs down with such a method of action.

1. We analyze our problem and break it down into steps so simple that we know we can master each step.

2. We can't assign each step of our problem to a different workman, but we can assign our undivided attention to the solution of each step.

When we concentrate our undivided attention on a single step, we can perform that step effectively and without error. We gain power just as a magnifying glass, by concentrating the rays of the sun on a single point, makes those rays extremely effective. In effect, we are using leverage, through specializing our activity.

We lose some of that power when we allow some of our attention to wander afield, just as a flaw in the magnifying glass would allow some of the concentrated effect of the rays of the sun to be scattered.

Our motivations command or drive us to act. We are all born with a set of basic motivations which drive us to do the things essential to living and reproduction. We call these basic motivations the physiological drives.

We have relatively few physiological drives. We have hunger, thirst, appetite, the sex drive, pain, fatigue, visceral tensions, sleepiness, warmth and cold, dryness and moisture, as related to the condition of our skin, air hunger, the exploratory drive, and possibly a couple of others that are debatable.

Yet there is no end to the number of motivations that we can build upon these drives, since motivations are built upon drives, and, in turn, other motivations are built upon these motivations. It often is difficult for us to see any relationship whatever between a motivation and the physiological drive from which it stems.

Although a motivation may be built upon a single drive, it is more likely to be built upon several, or even upon all of the drives, and most of our higher motivations are built upon hundreds of other motivations.

For instance, the desire to acquire money is founded on several drives, but we will consider its relation to the drive to seek food. We learn that money will buy food; thus money becomes a symbol representing food. Our drive to seek food may find an outlet through this specialized motivation to acquire money.

The drives themselves suffice for only our simpler acts. If the food is on the plate before us, then the physiological drive is effective enough. But when there is no food in sight, then the problem is more difficult—a specialized motivation helps us to concentrate our activity into a narrow, special field where it will be effective.

We learn that an educated man can earn more money, and earn it easier than an uneducated man; from the desire to acquire money springs the motivation to seek an education.

In the educational process we learn that we can learn easier if we co-operate. Thus from the desire to seek an education may spring the motivation to co-operate.

We learn that, if we try to please people, co-operation is more readily accomplished. Thus from the desire to cooperate may spring the motivation to develop a pleasing personality. Again and again we gain leverage through concentrating our activity in a special field.

As we build motivation upon motivation, we call the succeeding motivations our higher motivations. The motivations that are nearer to our physiological drives we call our lower motivations, with no reference to their moral values, though our higher motivations often seem to coincide with higher moral standards.

For simplification, we described a straight build-up, but the higher motivation may be, and almost always is, built upon a number of lower motivations, rather than one simply on top of another. Thus, the gregarious motivation is probably built upon a motivation to seek security, since there is safety in numbers; and upon the sex drive, since that drive could find no outlet if we lived alone.

But do you see what is happening? Each time we build a new motivation we are narrowing our field of activity; we are concentrating our actions into a special field where they will be more effective. The farther our motivations are removed from our physiological drives, the more they concentrate our activity; the more leverage they furnish us.

Consider the sex drive: The animals of the barnyard do not go through a very elaborate courtship but gain possession of the female through brute force, in which they often fight off other males in mortal combat. Man has learned that he can dispense with much of the wear and tear arising from combat with other males by influencing the female so that she will disregard other males in favor of him.

The desire to please and impress the female springs from the sex drive. Man also learns that the female wants a mate who will care for her in her pregnancy and who will help her to care for and rear her offspring. Hence, from the motivation to please and impress the female springs a motivation to become responsible.

We get leverage to make our action effective through specializing our activity in a narrow field through acting upon our higher motivations. Then why do we not act upon these higher motivations?

1. The higher motivation is indirect and often requires that we forego gratification at the moment for the sake of more certain gratification in the future. In other words, we suffer things which are at the moment unpleasant for the sake of more certain escape from these things in the future, or we put forth

effort now for future fulfillment.

2. The ability to do these things comes to us from a recognition of reality: through experience we recognize that we must sometimes endure things that are unpleasant, that we cannot always get things right now, and that we must make an effort now for the sake of future fulfillment.

When a child recognizes these facre of reality and shows a willingness to forego gratification at the moment for the sake of future gratification, it is making the first step toward adult behavior.

Sometimes we want things so badly right now that we act upon our lower motivations, which seem to present an opportunity for getting them right now. Thus, under the sex urge, the male may endeavor to possess the female through brutal, direct methods, instead of using the more certain and effective methods of courtship—he can't wait.

It must have been a great source of satisfaction when man first discovered that by placing a long pole under a huge boulder, with a small block under the pole near the boulder, he could easily move this giant boulder which a dozen men could not budge with their bare hands.

Yet, knowing this principle as we do, we often try to push the boulder with our bare hands; we scream and curse at it and beat at it with our fists, rather than searching for a lever with which we can effectively accomplish the job through the concentration of our efforts.

It is unfortunate that most of us think of patience as being slow or sluggish. Patient people can, and often do, act as quickly as or even quicker than the impatient. It is just that the patient individual goes in search of a lever with which to move the boulder instead of beating against it with his bare fists. He acts upon his higher motivations, because he has the ability to forego pleasure at the moment for the sake of future gratification. He doesn't waste energy in a frenzy of ineffective action.

The drive to do things or not to do them is our will. The

ability to direct this drive through our higher motivations, where it will be effective because it becomes specialized in a narrow radius of action, is our will power. It depends upon the ability to forego gratification at the moment for the sake of future gratification.

When we use will power we simply direct the commands arising from our physiological drives, through our higher motivations; using the longer levers we specialize.

Sometimes we try to act upon our higher motivations, then become so anxious to have things right now that we fall back to our lower motivations. Just as a mechanic, when he finds a nut too difficult to turn with his fingers, may use a wrench or a pair of pliers to get more leverage. Then, becoming impatient, he drops the wrench and struggles with the nut, using his fingers when it is still impossible to turn it effectively.

How can we develop will power?

1. By practice; by actually foregoing gratification for the moment; by actually putting forth effort for the sake of fulfillment.

2. By refusing to act upon lower motivations when we realize that the higher motivation will produce more certain results.

We use our powers of observation to ferret out these long levers. By concentrating our powers of observation into specialized fields, we discover means for directing our action into specialized fields.

The scientist concentrates his powers of observation on a tiny, specialized field by the use of the microscope.

We, however, are inclined to be impatient in using our powers of observation. We want to see everything at a glance. We dislike to search for details.

You are sitting in your airplane, revving up the motor. You simply listen to the loud roar, and it sounds all right to you. You motion to the mechanic to pull the chocks away from in front of the wheels. You are anxious to get into the air and on your way.

The mechanic strolls over to the side of the cockpit and says, "Hear that low thump-thump?" You listen and you detect it. "That," he says, "is probably a main bearing knock. Now, listen for that whistling, sucking hiss." You listen carefully and sure enough you hear it. "That," he points out, "is most likely a leak in the intake manifold."

You could have detected these things for yourself, but you were impatient to get into the air and wanted to hear it all in one quick instant.

We must be wary of individuals who appeal to us to use short levers, knowing that our intense desire to have things right now makes such an appeal effective.

Take the flamboyant advertiser: In a colorful, full-page advertisement, he portrays a glamorous movie star in all her beauty: a woman so beautiful that she has become the living symbol for beauty in the minds of millions of people. Then he simply has her saying, "I use Bunco Beauty Cream." That's all there is to it. You would like to be as beautiful as the movie star, and here is a nice, short lever. You can simply use Bunco Beauty Cream. No need to wait for future gratification; no need to work for fulfillment; you can get what you want right now.

The communist politician uses much the same method. He points out the luxuries which some of the tycoons of industry enjoy, and says, "Let's divide everything and then all of us can share these luxuries." Here is a short lever; a way to quick gratification, and we may be prone to seize upon it if we are not wary.

Now, if we concentrate our powers of observation into specialized aspects of the situation, what do we discover?

1. This industrial tycoon has been using a long lever himself. He has perfected some process which makes life fuller and richer for all of us. He has taken nothing from any of us but has merely profited from his ability to serve us better.

2. If we destroy him, we lower our own standard of living by depriving ourselves of the benefits of his efforts.

3. Divided among all of us, the spoils would be trifling as

compared to the service he renders us.

4. We will do better to develop some long levers to make our own action effective.

With no one encouraging us to do so, we continually grasp for these short levers. We don't like to make the effort to direct our powers of observation into specialized fields where we may discover longer levers which can make our action more effective. Unscrupulous individuals may capitalize upon this weakness, to cause us to act in a manner which will bring profit to them. We need not blind ourselves to the use of short levers. Use them where they will do the job, but learn to forego their use where they are not effective.

We are wise to use care in selecting the motivations upon which we act, the levers which we will use. For instance: The motivation to acquire money is only one of the levers available for our use in seeking food. It will not work in some circumstances.

Suppose you were shipwrecked, alone on a desert island. This motivation to acquire money would be a poor lever with which to seek food, since it would be concentrating your activity into a specialized field where, under the existing circumstances, it could not possibly produce results. You would quite likely starve to death if you dug for gold, instead of searching for food and doing some hunting and fishing.

Sometimes a particular lever works so well in so many circumstances that we become partial to it and may be tempted to use it in circumstances where it could not possibly produce results.

We also have to be wary of fashioning absurd levers, like a Rube Goldberg invention.

In solving our difficult problems, we break them down into easy steps, each one of which we can master. In effect, we use a series of long levers to reach our goal. The levers become a means to an end.

Mahatma Gandhi's entire life was dedicated to the principle: "The means is more important than the end." He believed that when we selected the wrong means to gain our end we either could not reach the end or we unconsciously, through these wrong motivations, changed our goal, so that when we reached it we had reached a different goal from the one for which we had originally headed.

Men who act effectively seem to have the ability to recognize their real goals. They select a series of long levers by means of which they may reach their ultimate goal—just as a skilled mechanic makes use of leverage furnished by wrenches.

Sometimes the ultimate goal seems so important to us that we are unable to transfer our attention from it to the means by which this ultimate end can be reached.

For instance: Your motor has suddenly stopped and all you can think of is the goal, the necessity for getting the airplane safely onto level ground while it is still in one piece.

You contemplate all the disastrous results that failure will produce, instead of directing your attention to the steps that you must follow in getting the airplane safely onto the ground. You neglect to use these long levers. You can think of nothing but your ultimate goal, and you can't wait to get there.

Suppose you break your problem down into steps A, B, C, D, and E, which are means to your end; the long levers you will use. Your success depends upon directing your attention to each step while you are performing that step.

Here is how we may fail: While we are working on Step A, that step doesn't seem so important because it is right here before us and we have our hands on it, in a position to do something about it. It doesn't seem so difficult, because we are in a position to accomplish it. But step B, step C, or any of the steps which lay ahead, are more elusive and may frighten us because they are not in our hands. We are in a hurry to get them and have them over with. While we are performing step A, part of our attention is on some future step, causing us to give step A insufficient attention and possibly to hurry it, with the result that we may not do it well.

Now when we reach this step which seemed so difficult, it

in turn doesn't seem so difficult as some other step which lies ahead. Again we divide our attention, looking ahead to a step which we are not performing. Moreover, since we most likely have made a mistake in performing step A, we may still further divide our attention by worrying about the mistake we made.

Is it any wonder that such a procedure results in ineffective action?

Certainly we have to plan ahead; there are details of each step that must be planned in advance. Bear in mind, however, that this planning itself is but one intermediate step of the long series, each step of which must be performed in turn if we are to reach our goal successfully.

It is unfortunate that we think of patience as such a dull quality when it is the quality that underlies our ability to keep our attention directed to the step at hand.

When we encounter in our path a small boulder that we can easily move with our hands, we would be foolish to go in search of a lever with which to move it more easily. We move it with our hands because it is quicker—short levers where they can do the job always get quicker action than long levers. That is why we are so fond of them and like to use them in preference to long levers. But when we encounter a boulder in our path which we cannot budge with our bare hands, then we should go in search of a lever with which to move it effectively.

By continually using long levers where they are more effective, we develop a habit of using long levers; we develop the ability to forego gratification when we see it is impossible to get gratification instantly. We concentrate our efforts into a specialized field, where they will be more effective and thus more certain of fulfilling our desires. We are willing to wait and work for this more certain gratification. That in essence is will power, the ability to direct our will into narrow channels, wherein our efforts are more effective because they are specialized.

For all of us, there are things that we need, things that we wish to possess, and things that we wish to accomplish. Those are our goals. When those goals cannot be quickly attained by direct methods, we approach them indirectly. Through the use of our intellectual powers we break down the attainment of our goals into easy steps. These steps become the means—the levers by which we make our action so effective that we can eventually reach our goal.

Our dominating motivation is to reach our goal, but we develop supporting motivations, long levers by means of which we accomplish this end. It is important that we act upon these higher motivations and that we use these long levers in order to accomplish our purpose.

All of men's mechanical success has been made possible through the use of levers, of which the wheel is one modified form. The lever is a fitting symbol for that rare ability that enables man to perform seemingly impossible tasks and to reach far-flung goals.

This ability enables him to concentrate his activity in specialized fields so that it becomes effective. In the development of this ability lies the key to the power and the strength with which to make our actions effective and our lives successful.

Made in the USA
San Bernardino, CA
12 December 2016